To my bride and my lover, Tiffani. Your unwavering support and belief in me has made me a better man; I am truly better because of you. I love you!

UNSATISFIED

WHEN LESS IS MORE

MATTHEW Q. LESSER

UNSATISFIED
When Less Is More

ISBN HARDCOVER: 978-1-5445-3548-7
      PAPERBACK: 978-1-5445-3546-3
      EBOOK: 978-1-5445-3547-0

CONTENTS

FOREWORD

By Chuck Bentley

LEADERSHIP COACHING, PERSONAL development, and executive consulting is a crowded space. Over the years, I have engaged with a variety of programs promising to enhance my progress as a leader. I can count on one hand those that I would recommend to others. The most common shortcomings of the programs I engaged with were a) the approach was based on a formula or steps that failed to get into my real challenges—those that reside inside my heart and mind—or b) the life experience of the coach was simply lacking, leaving a shallow well of practical experience and knowledge to draw from.

Matt Lesser has created a training model and approach for personal growth forged from his broad, deep, personal, and often painful real-life experience. He did not find a one-size-fits-all formula to go to market with a prepackaged plan to launch a second career. He suffered through times of emotional overload, exhausting periods of striving, and seasons of outward thriving marked by frustrating emptiness that caused him to wrestle through his search for that elusive goal of flourishing inwardly and outwardly, at home and at work.

Let's be honest; we have all been there in some aspect or the other. Who has not sensed that you were climbing the wrong ladder, aiming at the wrong target, achieving an unfulfilling goal, feeling anxious and empty, and yearning for a more meaningful life? I certainly have, which is why I appreciate Matt's willingness to be frank about his own experience by mapping out the journey that brought him to the point of discovering and applying what is needed to become integrated as a husband, father, and business leader. His passion is to guide others to experience what few leaders ever do—a deep sense of joy and satisfaction with all aspects of life.

Get ready to discover your purpose, your true core, and the joy of less becoming more.

CHUCK BENTLEY

June 2022

INTRODUCTION

ARE YOU SATISFIED?
 I don't mean the kind of satisfaction you feel after a good meal where you push back from the table and the only thing you can think of is having a nice long nap. I mean the kind of long-lasting satisfaction that perseveres through the ups and downs, mountain tops and valleys of life. We live in a world where we're bombarded with commercials, social media, and other advertisements telling you that you need *more* and *better* to find satisfaction. But how do you find this contentment or satisfaction? They'll tell you the answers are *more* and *better*. *Better*: you need a *better* job, a *better* vehicle, or a *better* house. *More*: you need *more* money, *more* clothes, or *more* power. It is only with *more* and *better* that you can truly experience satisfaction. That is the message our society sends to you.

So are you satisfied with your job? How about your car? Your home? Your savings account? Your 401(k)? Your weight? Your spouse? Your life? I hypothesize that you would answer, "Yes...and no," because you probably experience both satisfaction and unsatisfaction in these areas of your life. But have you ever stopped to think about that word: *satisfied*?

What do we do with our lives because of this messaging? So many people—myself included—spend so much of life pursuing what we think will make us satisfied and happy: Career. Money. Power. Houses. Cars. Education. Certifications. Titles. Rank. Position. Place. Experiences. Relationships. Reputation. Expertise. We pursue all these things and so much more in a pursuit to find meaning, purpose, fulfillment, and satisfaction in life.

We believe we are pursuing a satisfied life, but even when we do accumulate *more*, and we have *better*, it leaves us feeling empty and *unsatisfied*. Why? Because none of these bring lasting satisfaction, only temporary satisfaction. We spend so much of our lives trying to become something we are not—or trying to emulate someone else's life because we falsely believe their lives are better than our own. We hop onto the treadmill of life and start playing the "If Only" game. *If only I made more money. If only I had a bigger house. If only I had a better job.* You get where I am going. We run ourselves ragged chasing after the next "If Only," just to find that once we get that raise, promotion, bigger house, new car, or advanced degree, the satisfaction we desire—that we crave—is short-lived at best but mostly just hollow and empty.

Let me ask you a question: What would it feel like if you were *satisfied*—truly satisfied? What would it be like to know that you were living a life of purpose, meaning, and satisfaction? Is it even possible to live like this? Is it possible to *not* be exhausted all the time because you are working so much to prove your worth or working overtime to make as much additional money as possible? Is it possible to be content and satisfied with what you currently own, rather than having more, the newer, the better, the bigger? Is it possible to be both physically available to your family (because you are not working all the time or always on your phone answering emails and text messages) and emotionally available to your family (because you are not so stressed out all the time thinking about work)?

If you have given up hope thinking that there is another way to live, let me be the first to share this truth with you: there is a way to live a *satisfied* life! How? By getting to the heart of the matter—the root cause of what is making you feel *unsatisfied* to begin with. That is the purpose of this book.

I lived the first forty-seven years of my life chasing *more* and *better*. Let me give you a handful of quick-hit examples of what I mean (I will unpack this in more detail in Part II). In school, from elementary all the way through graduate school, getting an A was never good enough for me. I had to have the A+. I spent the first fifteen years in the business world building my family business into *more* and *better*. When I sold the family businesses, I went into the world of private equity. I focused on *more* and *better* in every role I had for the twelve years I was there as I sought to climb the proverbial corporate ladder, gaining more responsibility and earning more money along the way.

In my never-ending search for *more* and *better*, I left my senior executive role in private equity and entered the banking world as a senior executive. I stayed for less than one year because I knew my quest for more would not be satisfied there. I left the banking world and joined a friend as part of his executive team, helping him chase *his* dream of building his family business to *more* and *better*. After several months, we accomplished the goal of restructuring, and my role changed. I knew I would not find satisfaction in that new role.

I left that role, and I started my own training and consulting business focused on leadership development, team building, executive coaching, writing, and speaking, which is now my profession. So did I suddenly stop pursuing *more* and *better* when I started my own business? I stopped pursuing *more* and *better* as an ends unto themselves, and I started pursuing *meaning*, *purpose*, and *impact* instead. If my business leads to *more* and *better*, then so be it; however, they are no longer what motivate or drive me because now I realize that *more* and *better* are never satisfied—they only lead you to want to have even *more* and *better*.

Before launching my business, I took some time off (they call that a "career break" these days) to look inward and around me because I knew my life had stopped working. Everything stopped working. I will share more of my story in Part II, but it is important that I share the context of my story with you up front so you know who I am and why I authored this book. By nature, I am a driven, bottom-line, get-it-done, no-nonsense personality type who gets much satisfaction and much of my identity out of being able to get large volumes of tasks done with satisfactory results. Whether in my work or volunteering at church, Little League coaching, leading a small group, preaching and teaching, speaking, having a book study, or mentoring guys along the way, I did life the only way I knew how: all-in, break-neck speed, large volume, and results-oriented. I had a terrible time saying no to anything anyone asked of me. Why? Because I believed that if *some* is good, then *more* must be better, right? And for the first forty-seven years of my life, this is how I lived.

Was my life terrible? No. However, I was beginning to drive those closest in my life away from me in my relentless pursuit of *more* and *better*, and I did not begin to realize this until it was too late. It was not until I intentionally took time off and began to do serious introspection and pay attention to what was happening around me that my eyes began to open. The truth is that my way of doing life began to break five years prior to my realizing that it wasn't working. How did I finally know that my life broke and that it had stopped working? Because that is when I began to think and dream about life looking and functioning much differently, radically differently. I began to dream of life with *less*: *less* commitments, *less* responsibilities, *less* time away, *less* possessions, *less* stress, *less* money. I began dreaming of selling everything, moving to a remote part of the world, and living as a hermit with little to no contact with the outside world for the rest of my days. In addition to dreaming of living as a hermit, I also began to work on the model that is now in this book you are reading or listening to.

Over much of my career, I have had the wonderful opportunity to travel to many countries and meet and work with amazing leaders—leaders of business, nonprofit organizations, government, NGOs, churches, and academia. As I collaborated with these leaders and examined my own life, I began to realize that many of those leaders shared the same motivation and drive that I had—the pursuit of *more* and *better*. Why? To find meaning, purpose, and satisfaction in life. The sad reality is that, like me, many of those leaders lived in the daily tension of being *unsatisfied* while pursuing, day after day, what we thought would bring satisfaction...*more* and *better*. The problem with pursuing satisfaction with *more* and *better*, I have come to realize, is this: *more* and *better* can never be satisfied—that leads only to *unsatisfaction* because there is always "more" on top of *more* and a "better" *better*. Instead, the answer lies much deeper within at the core of who we are as human beings, created by a loving God, living in a world where everyone is desperately trying to find meaning and purpose in life. So what is the answer to the ubiquitous problem of being *unsatisfied*? Making the intentional choice to pursue a *flourishing* life instead: where pursuing *less* is actually *more*.

During the last four jobs I held in the marketplace, I was *thriving* on the outside, but I was barely *surviving* on the inside. Only a few people—people who knew me and loved me well—knew it. Those jobs were all high-level, senior/executive leadership positions (i.e., in the family businesses, private equity, banking, and industrial services). A reasonable person who did not know me and was on the outside looking in would look at me and these roles and easily conclude that I was *thriving*—even *flourishing*—in those roles and in life in general. In addition to having high-level leadership positions, I was also in several other senior-level leadership positions in other organizations I served—my church, board of director roles on over a dozen boards both domestically and internationally, and I was asked to speak several times a year at events ranging from church services to motivational keynotes, to the classroom, to inspirational events for different organizations. But the reality was different. I had a great "game face," and I knew how to wear it well to disguise the reality that underneath the mask, I was barely holding on—I was barely *surviving.*

> **How about you? Do you have a good "game face" on? Do the people you work with every day think you are thriving, while you are barely surviving on the inside? If something comes to mind, write it down so you have it with you. We will spend time unpacking what to do with what you wrote down in Part III.**

Throughout the book, I will pose these "How about you?" questions to provoke you to think about how this book and the lessons it contains can apply to your own life. I encourage you to pause when you come to these "How about you?" moments. And if you enjoy keeping a journal or if you think more clearly when you are writing, I also encourage you to have paper and pen ready as you read this book. When you come to these questions, take a few moments, write down the question, and then write your answer by applying the questions to your own life, story, or journey. The power in reading any book is not in the words and the information you are reading; it is in the application and the integration of the information into your own life. If you are like me, I enjoy reading a book as fast as possible from cover to cover, and the thought of stopping to answer questions can be annoying; however, the older I get, the more I understand and accept the wisdom in taking time to ponder, think, apply, practice, and integrate new information and learning into my own life and story. So I encourage you to pause, ponder, apply, and integrate the questions throughout this book into your story and journey in whatever way or ways (e.g., journaling, closing your eyes and meditating, thinking for a few moments) you best learn and integrate new information into your life.

Returning to the story, my epiphany moment came after I was invited to join an international community of leaders that gathered once per year for fellowship, relationship building, and engaging discussions on important topics. The price for admission to the annual event was to write and submit a "white paper" of an original idea. The second year I attended this event, I authored a paper that I put into the form of a letter to my oldest son. On the final night of the event, I was presented with an amazingly humbling award: my paper was voted the best paper of the conference that year. As I walked off the stage after receiving my award, I had two thoughts go through my head. First thought: *This is what I was called to do when I was a teenager.* Second thought: *I have to go back to work tomorrow.* The first thought gave me unbelievable joy, excitement, and hope. The second thought gave me huge anxiety, caused me to lose hope, and made me want to throw up.

How about you? Does the thought of going to work tomorrow give you joy, excitement, and hope? Or does the thought of going to work tomorrow want to make you throw up and give you anxiety? If anything comes to mind, write it down or remember it later when we arrive at Part III in our journey together.

I am here to tell you that you do not have to live this way! There is another way to live that is freeing, hope-filled, and so much better than living with the nightly dread of having to wake up and go to a job that you hate going to. Is it easy to live this way? I wish there were an uncomplicated way to live life. There is not; however, there is a way to live life that will make it so much more fulfilling and satisfying than what you may be experiencing now.

How do you get that life? By making intentional choices on how you want to live your life's journey! It starts by acknowledging and accepting that the life you have been living is not working—at least not working how you thought it would work or how you thought it was supposed to work. The key word is *intentional*: intentionally choosing to live the kind of life you want to live. Life happens, and life continues regardless of whether or not you're making intentional choices.

How about you? Are you living your life intentionally or unintentionally? The choice is up to you.

This book is all about intentionality and choosing to live your life with purpose, on purpose, and for purpose—intentionally. Once you acknowledge and accept reality, then you are ready to move on and learn about what it means to live a *flourishing* life and intentionally choosing to pursue *less* so that you can experience *more* in life.

Eric Liddell is an example of intentionally pursuing *less* to experience *more*. He is the subject of one of my favorite movies of all time, "Chariots of Fire."[1] It is not my favorite because of the story of the two runners—both of whom thrived in their running careers. Rather, I have been an enthusiastic fan of Eric's ever since I first

---

1   *Chariots of Fire*, directed by Hugh Hudson, written by Colin Welland, and produced by David Puttnam (London: Enigma Productions, 1981).

heard about him, then read books about him, and then watched the movie. As I studied his life, there was only one thing that was more important to Eric than running, and that was his faith. Eric's unwillingness to compromise his core beliefs of not competing on a Sunday—even in the Olympic finals—was so intriguing to me that his story captured my imagination. I had to know more about this man. The more I learned about Eric Liddell, the more I began to see a pattern in Eric's life. And this pattern was the initial spark that lit a fire in me to author this book.

Without Eric's story, I am not sure I would have authored this book. Learning about one man who was willing to sacrifice Olympic history, stardom, fame, and monetary award (although not as lucrative as today's modern-day athletes enjoy) for something that was even more important to him, intrigued and inspired me. Eric was quoted once as saying, "I believe that God made me for a purpose, but He also made me fast! And when I run fast, I feel His pleasure."[2] This quote not only captured my imagination, but it also messed with my head for years.

I desperately wanted to "experience God's pleasure" in what I did, but it was not until I was well into my forty-seventh year of life that I finally experienced what Eric Liddell referred to. I was facilitating a group of about twenty senior leaders at a large nonprofit organization close to where I lived. They had invited me to come in and help them better understand who they were—both as individuals and as a team. I had the team complete one of my favorite assessments prior to our time together, and then I facilitated the time with them by reviewing their results. We discussed the strengths and weaknesses of the team and the growth areas and blind spots over four hours together (we had allotted two

---

2   Eric Liddell, *The Disciplines of the Christian Life* (Nashville: Abingdon Press, 1985).

hours—we decided to work through lunch!). I walked out of that engagement, got into my truck, shut the door, and then it hit me. A wave of emotion swept over me out of nowhere, and I wept—and I am not an emotional guy (for years, my wife has said I am emotionally constipated, and I have wondered myself if my tear ducts even worked!)—I literally wept in my truck for the next fifteen to twenty minutes. Why did I weep? Because I felt it...*I felt God's pleasure*. For four hours that morning, I was doing exactly what God created, equipped, trained, and prepared me to do. I did not realize it until I sat in my truck, and then I knew it—*I felt God's pleasure*. For context, at the time, I was nearing the end of my last executive role, where my role had changed, and I was struggling with that role. This was truly a gift from God.

I believe that God genuinely wants us to live life to the fullest and experience all that life has to offer—a life of joy and satisfaction. So how do Eric Liddell's story, my story, and your story all intersect? By all definitions, Eric Liddell experienced *thriving* as a runner. If Eric Liddell thrived as a runner, then what could be more important than experiencing a life of *thriving*? Why was he seemingly *unsatisfied* and wanting something else? It was this question that drove me and motivated me to search deeper. For Eric Liddell, this is what motivated him to pursue something other than *thriving* when he ran:

> It has been a wonderful experience to compete in the Olympic Games and to bring home a gold medal. But since I have been a young lad, I have had my eyes on a different prize. You see, each one of us is in a greater race than any I have run in Paris, and this race ends when God gives out the medals.[3]

---

3   Source widely attributed to Eric Liddell.

Eric Liddell experienced *thriving* when he ran, but he experienced *flourishing* when he had his eyes on this "different prize" that was his greater and truer calling (I will give more definition and clarity on "calling" in Chapter 2) as a human being. For me, I experienced a *thriving* life many times and in many roles, but living a *thriving* life did not provide me with lasting satisfaction, only temporary. I was still *unsatisfied.*

How about you? When have you felt or experienced a sense of being *unsatisfied*?

I believe we all experience moments of being *satisfied*—like when we attain a goal, obtain a victory, accomplish what we set out to accomplish, or our boss acknowledges that we did excellent work and compliments us. Most of these moments of satisfaction are fleeting, and soon, you are back on the treadmill of life pursuing the next goal, task, *more, better, bigger,* or whatever drives you to find satisfaction. This book, *unSatisfied: When Less Is More,* is all about unpacking the journey to live your life intentionally pursuing lasting satisfaction.

Eric Liddell may have served as a source of inspiration and motivation for me to write this book, but there are hundreds, probably thousands, of other examples of people who, by any definition, were experiencing a *thriving* life and intentionally chose to set that aside for something greater—something more meaningful, a greater calling, a greater purpose—for a life that is *flourishing.* Are you as intrigued as I was when I learned about *thriving* versus *flourishing*?

One of my favorite questions to ask people, especially when I am coaching them, is this: *What points of pain are you currently experiencing?* It is these "points of pain," then, that we focus on in our coaching times together to think through, evaluate, and solve the pain.

How about you? What are the points of pain in your life?

This book is a journey for you, but I will be with you every step of the way as you turn the pages of this book. On this journey, I will share with you a model—the Flourishing Life Model—of how you, too, can make the choice to live a *flourishing* life, where pursuing *less* is actually *more*. The model is a triangle comprised of five levels. The five levels are mirrors for you in your journey where you can identify points of pain in your life, pause for self-reflection, and grow in self-awareness. The model is intended to be used as a holistic evaluation of your life, as in, which level do you view yourself being in as a whole person? It is also intended to be used to evaluate your life by the various roles you have in your own life's journey. To put it more simply, the Flourishing Life Model is intended to be used by *role* and *as a whole* in your journey toward making the intentional choices to live a *flourishing* life.

Along the journey, I will provide you with as many tools and evaluation "lenses" as possible so you can evaluate your life as thoroughly as you desire. For example, at the risk of alienating you, the reader, I decided to include the characteristic of "spiritual" as one of the characteristics to be evaluated. Some readers will be interested in the spiritual dimension because it is a big part of who they are. The spiritual dimension of life is especially important to me, but that does not mean it is or must be a core dimension for you. I hope it is because I care about you, and I believe that the more thorough and holistic you are in how you self-evaluate, the more opportunity you have to become the best version of who you can become.

I understand that any use of words pertaining to "spiritual," "God," or "Jesus" can cause discomfort for some, so please hear my heart before deciding whether or not to continue reading. I am a believer in Jesus, and I have a personal relationship with Him. I desire to live every day in such a way as to practically demonstrate His love and His character to the world around me. Do I do this perfectly? Absolutely not. I fail every day, which is why I need His forgiveness and His grace. I do not consider myself to be religious because I believe religion is man-made, and I have observed and experienced way too many awful, dreadful, hurtful, devastating things done in the name of "religion." I am all about a relationship with a loving God who loved me when I was not even capable of understanding His love or loving Him in return. I want to be honest and truthful with you, which is why I am sharing my perspective in the beginning pages of this book. I promise not to evangelize or proselytize you on our journey together. I will occasionally share how God has worked in my life because God is part of who I am; however, when I do share, I am not telling you that you also have to have God in your life—I am simply sharing my journey with you.

It is time for a moment of transparent truth with you—from my heart to yours: the last thing I want and the last thing you need is to read another book that is so esoteric and complex that you have to buy a companion guide to explain the book to you. (Kind of like the old *CliffsNotes* versions to complex or long topics that I used to use in college—as a side note, I thought that *CliffsNotes* were amazing. I would not have survived at least four college classes without them!) I also do not want this book to turn into another shelf-sitting dust collector. I want you, at some point in your onward journey, to look back at the time you invested in reading this book—yes, the words you are reading or listening to right now—and say, "That book made a difference in my life!"

Before we launch, I want to show you the map of our journey. I will first provide definitions and discuss both the barriers and accelerators at each level of the model in Part I. In Part II, I will then share with you some additional details of my own journey to provide you with insights that you can apply to your life and provide hope that there is another way to live than being perpetually *unsatisfied* with your life. Last, in Part III, I will conclude our journey together by offering you practical ways you can integrate and apply the model to your life by offering exercises, assessments to help you grow in self-awareness, and coaching that has been critical for me as I have learned how to live my life more intentionally focused on *flourishing*. That is the overview of the map of our journey together through the pages of this book. Are you ready to embark on our journey together? Let's go!

To start, let's jump into the Flourishing Life Model.

PART I

THE MODEL: THE FLOURISHING LIFE MODEL

CHAPTER 1

In the Zone

THINK BACK. REFLECT. When was a time in your life when you knew—you *just knew*—you were "in the zone"? You were "hitting on all cylinders," you were on "cruise control," and you had the audience "eating out of the palm of your hand." It seemed like you were hitting everything pitched to you, and you were hitting it out of the park. It appeared you could do no wrong, and people around you noticed it as well. You were loving it, and you wished it would never end.

It may have been that important high-profile project where you were hoping to be asked to be the team lead. When the day and time came, you got the call, and your boss asked you to do just that. You not only did it, but you also delivered it ahead of schedule, under budget, your team was energized and engaged, and you knew—you *just knew*—that you came through with excellence.

Or the time you were asked to tag along on a weeklong trip to a developing country. You did not really want to go at first; however, after a couple of days in the field, engaging with the people and serving them with food and medical supplies, something began to tug at your heart. And when you returned home, all you could think about was the next time you would be able to go back and see your new friends again in that country.

Maybe it was the time you were asked to organize the supply closet—you know, the closet that no one would ever go near because they never knew if they would ever find their way back out, and you were convinced that last summer's interns were still lost in there somewhere. You have a natural gift for organizing and making sense of chaos. Even though the project seemed menial, when you finished, you felt amazing, and it seemed like everyone—even the CEO of the company—thought you were a rock star because no one needed to be afraid of the supply closet any longer.

How about you? What and when have you experienced success that was beyond success—success that was wrapped in meaning, purpose, and fulfillment beyond what you had ever experienced before? When you begin to identify those experiences in your life, you are beginning to understand what flourishing is all about.

I have used the terms *thriving* and *flourishing.* Let's examine the difference. Remember when I said that Eric Liddell experienced *thriving* when he ran, but he *flourished* when he had his eyes on a "different prize" he referred to as his greater and truer calling as a human being? You'll need to understand both, so let's compare and contrast the meaning of *thriving* and *flourishing* to give us a baseline of understanding. I will define *flourishing* in the next chapter, but *thriving* means to "grow vigorously or gain in wealth or possessions; to prosper."[4]

---

4   *Merriam-Webster.com Dictionary*, s.v. "thrive (*v.*)," accessed August 3,

If *thriving* means "to gain in wealth or possessions," then money must truly be the answer to happiness, fulfillment, and satisfaction. But wait. It isn't, is it? Why? If the accumulation of money, wealth, power, and possessions was the answer, then wouldn't the world's richest, most famous, and most powerful be the ultimate examples and role models of what it means to live a full and meaningful life? A life that is fulfilled and satisfied? But it seems that all you must do is look at the news headlines on any given day and read or hear about yet another example of the world's richest, most famous, and most powerful who behaved badly, ruined their marriages, or compromised their reputations for what—*more* money? *More* power? I don't believe so. I believe it is because they lack something—something in their core, something deep within them that they may not even be able to identify or define. And here is the rub with *thriving*: by its very definition, *thriving* is **never satisfied**—it leads to a life that is *unsatisfied*.

Arthur Brooks, author of *The Atlantic*, says this when it comes to satisfaction:

> Time and again, I have fallen into the trap of believing that success and its accompaniments would fulfill me. On my 40th birthday I made a bucket list of things I hoped to do or achieve. There were accomplishments only a wonk could want: writing books and columns about serious subjects, teaching at a top school, traveling to give lectures and speeches, maybe even leading a university or think tank. Whether these were good and noble goals or not, they were my goals, and I imagined that if I hit them, I would be satisfied. I found that list nine years ago, when I was forty-eight, and realized that

2022, https://www.merriam-webster.com/dictionary/thrive.

I had achieved every item on it. I had been a tenured professor, then the president of a think tank. I was giving frequent speeches, had written some books that had sold well, and was writing columns for the New York Times. But none of that had brought me the lasting joy I had envisioned. Each accomplishment thrilled me for a day or a week—a month, never more—and then I reached for the next rung on the ladder.[5]

John Ortberg authored a book several years ago that captured my imagination when I read it because of the simple yet profound way he summarized life. The name of the book is *When the Game Is Over, It All Goes Back in the Box.*[6] In his book, John paints the picture that at the end of our lives, everything we have worked hard for and accumulated—whether a little or a lot—all goes back in the box. As I read this book, it was as if John himself kept reaching out of his book, thumping me on the forehead, and saying, "Yes, I am talking to you, dummy!" It is so easy, especially in Western culture, to get caught up in the game of thinking that life is all about accumulating things and that the more we accumulate, the more we are winning the game.

I remember seeing a T-shirt when I was a kid that said, "He who dies with the most toys...wins!" Unfortunately, that is a cultural lie that we are fed from the time we can understand the meaning of words. We take nothing with us out of this life. We go into a box, and the game is over. I wish that T-shirt had said, "He who dies

---

5   Arthur C. Brooks, *From Strength to Strength: Finding Success, Happiness, and Deep Purpose in the Second Half of Life* (New York: Portfolio/Penguin, 2022).

6   John Ortberg, *When the Game Is Over, It All Goes Back in the Box* (Grand Rapids, MI: Zondervan, 2007).

with the most toys...still dies!" because that is the truth. The older I get, the more I realize how true this statement really is, which is why I am convinced that *thriving* falls woefully short of describing the life that we should aspire to achieve. Because to describe someone as *thriving*, by dictionary or societal definition, is incomplete and empty. *Thriving* focuses on *more* and *better*—a focus internally on getting what is mine and getting all I can get while I can get it—which is never satisfied. *Flourishing*, on the other hand, is a focus on *meaning* and *purpose*—a focus externally on what I can give and contribute, making an impact, and living a life with purpose, for purpose, and on purpose—which leads to lasting satisfaction.

If *thriving* is incomplete to describe the secret to a life that is full, fulfilled, and satisfied, then what is the answer? More importantly, how do you get there? Although there is no special formula, secret pathway, or shortcut on this journey, there is a legitimate and reasonable journey to be considered. Is it easy? No, or everyone would be doing it. Is it simple? Yes, but simple to understand rarely translates into simple to execute. I am not saying that *thriving* is unimportant because I believe that it is an important part of the journey to go on. So if thriving is important but there is something more important than *thriving*, what should we aspire to? What should we focus on to pursue a life of meaning, purpose, fullness, and satisfaction? The answer is to pursue a *flourishing* life, which is what the next chapter is all about.

.

CHAPTER 2

Burn the Ships

I N 1519, HERNÁN Cortés sailed from Spain to the New World with a fleet of ships. When they arrived in the New World, Cortés's men faced all kinds of hardships, diseases, and the unknown. They became afraid and threatened mutiny, leaving Cortés behind (or killing him), and returning to Spain. Cortés became aware of the plans of his crew and, one day, had them all go to shore. When his men were on shore, he burned all the ships—literally set fire to the entire fleet and destroyed all the ships. Now Cortés and his men had no choice: they had to figure out how to survive in this new land...or die. Cortés created a point of no return for himself and his men. As a result of removing the option to return to Spain, Cortés and his men figured out how to survive, they conquered the new land, and they established their own colony in the New World. Since 1519, the phrase "Burn the ships" has become synonymous with removing all options except moving forward, of being "all-in," and of not turning back.

How about you? What have you faced in your life where you had to decide that turning back was no longer an option for you, so you "burned the ships" and moved forward—directly into the face of fear, anxiety, the unknown, obstacles, and an unclear path?

It is not easy, is it? However, knowing that you are "all-in" and blazing a new path brings a level of excitement and hope that you may have never experienced before. It is this excitement, the pursuit of a dream or the pursuit of what you are passionate about, that provides the motivation, the courage, and the perseverance to go on—and stay on—the journey toward choosing a life that is *flourishing*.

If *flourishing* is the ultimate goal, then let's define what that means. According to Webster, *flourishing* means "to grow or develop in a healthy or vigorous way."[7] As I looked for deeper definitions and practical examples of *flourishing* in literature, articles, research, and periodicals, I found a common thread. *Flourishing* in much of modern-day literature emphasizes the importance of providing the world, especially the developing world, with the opportunity to live without the day-to-day pressure to survive without facing starvation, debilitating illnesses, disease, or natural disasters. *Flourishing* in literature often seeks to address poverty, starvation, and disease in the parts of the world that are severely impoverished and disadvantaged. Although I am presenting a different application for the meaning of the word *flourishing* in this book, I do not seek to diminish the amazing effort, work, and focus of those people and organizations that are laser-focused on

---

7   *Merriam-Webster.com Dictionary*, s.v. "flourishing (*adj.*)," accessed August 3, 2022, https://www.merriam-webster.com/dictionary/flourishing.

addressing the systemic issues, tragedies, and problems to solve that we face in this world.

For our purposes, *flourishing* is not just about success in a career or the accumulation of money, possessions, power, or wealth—these are the focus of *thriving*. *Flourishing* is about more than these—it transcends. *Flourishing* is not a feeling or a definition. *Flourishing* is also not just in the mind. *Flourishing* means to live at the intersection of four components: what you are passionate about, what you are gifted and good at doing, what others confirm and affirm that you contribute to them, and what you feel called to do in life. *Thriving*, I contend, is the intersection of two or three of these but not all four. What do I mean? I simply mean this: once you get a taste of what it means to flourish, you will know it, and you will never want to taste anything else! The graphic below illustrates this.

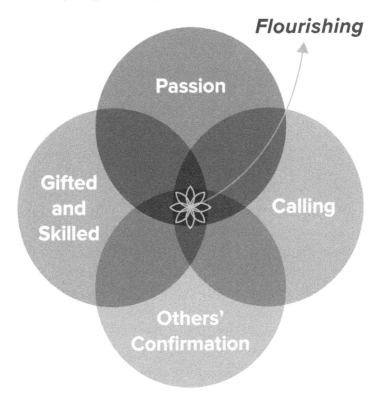

One's "calling" can be a difficult concept to understand, so think of it this way: what you believe is one of the primary reasons you are on this earth. It may be something that you have wanted to do since you were a kid. How many people do you know who wanted to be a firefighter, a police officer, or an airplane pilot since they could first speak? This gets to the essence of *calling*. From a spiritual perspective, "calling" comes from understanding one's "being" (or identity, as God created that person) and understanding one's "belonging" in a relationship with a loving God who created that person. It is out of this *being* and *belonging* that a person grows to understand and have the clarity to discern what God has "called" that person to then do. *Calling* may not be doing just one thing for the rest of your life; it could change or modify over your life's journey, just as you change, grow, and mature.

In my own journey to *flourishing*, I had to "burn the ships," fully knowing the path would be anything but easy. The journey to *flourishing* is not easy, nor is it a straight-line journey. It is often filled with obstacles, potholes, and detours (as my story is, and I am sure your story is as well); however, it is an intentional journey that you can choose to take by deciding that is what you desire to pursue in life.

Personally, whenever I embark on a journey or I commit myself to something, I want to know the answers to three questions: (1) What? (2) Why? and (3) How? The most important is knowing the why. It is important for us to pause for a moment and examine these three questions briefly. I will start with why since it is most important.

Why is this model important, and *why* is it something to consider? The answer is best answered individually because each person reading this will arrive at their own why answer. A simple, high-level answer is, this model works to compel and motivate you to intentionally choose a life that is *flourishing*. I have a tough time accepting or believing in something that does not work. *Why* does it work? Because I have lived long enough to observe many others' lives and long enough to know for me, personally, that pursuing a *thriving* life as our culture has defined it leads to a life that is empty and wanting. It is *not* a full life. It is an *unsatisfied* life. The why for me is easy: I do not want to spend any more of my life pursuing things that I know will bring me temporary happiness, unsatisfaction, and long-term emptiness, and I do not want anyone else to experience this either. My hope and prayer for you as you read this book is that you walk away from this book with a renewed hope that you can live life in an intentional way to bring lasting fulfillment, joy, and satisfaction. You may have lived a life that, until now, has experienced a lack of fulfillment, a lack of joy, or *unsatisfaction*—regardless of how long you have lived. The good news is, there is another way to live that has a much better opportunity to bring fulfillment, joy, and satisfaction.

I view life as a journey and as a book that is written with each day we live. If you look back on the book of your life—written up until now—and you do not like the book you have written, you have a choice you can make. Moreover, you can make it right now. You can put a period on the page and the chapter you are currently writing; you can turn to a new page, and you can start authoring your book with a whole new ending. You cannot rewrite what you have already written because it is part of the story of your life; however, you get to choose how the book will end. Please do not misread this: I am not saying that you may not like everything that you have written; there are most likely some amazing chapters written in your life's book! I would only ask you to evaluate the book you are currently writing and the ending that will most likely come because of the book in progress. Will it be the ending you want to write? If it is, then wonderful—keep writing! If it is not, put down a period, turn the page, and start writing the book that will have the ending you intentionally desire. That is the power of why.

Now the what. *What* is this model all about, and where did it come from? The model is about showing a journey that most, if not all, of us go on in life. As I unpack the model, I think this will become more clearly defined. There are areas in your life where you may currently be experiencing or have experienced living a *diminished* existence. There are areas where you are *surviving*— barely *surviving* but *surviving*, nonetheless. There are areas where you are *striving*—*striving* to achieve more, *striving* to become something else, *striving* to thrive. There are areas where you are *thriving*—*thriving* because you are experienced, gifted, or skilled at something; *thriving* because you are good at doing something. And there are areas where you are *flourishing*—*flourishing* by living at the intersection of what you are good at doing, passionate about doing, making a difference in others' lives, and called to (and loving) whatever it is you are doing. The model came from years of talking with people, coaching leaders, reading, studying, researching, and experiencing these stages myself.

What about how? *How* do you use the model? This is where you may or may not like my answer. *How* you use the model completely depends on how *you WANT* to use the model. Clear as mud? I am kidding. The model is not meant to be a solution—it is meant to be a way for you to see your journey and your story in such a way as to bring clarity to your personal purpose and reason for existence in this life. The model is meant to help you find *satisfaction* in life amid all the *unsatisfaction* that you may have experienced. The model is intended to be part of your journey—both now and into the future. In Part III of this book, I will better answer the question of how as I show you how to integrate the model into your life so you are equipped to intentionally choose a *flourishing* life or not, because it is your life and your choice!

With that as the foundation and lead-in to the model, let's jump into the model. After we explore the model, I will share my own personal story to show that there is a path to *flourishing* even during difficulty, pain, failures, hardship, and setbacks and to encourage you to use your voice and share your own story. Finally, we will wrap things up by exploring how we can all effectively and simply use the model to integrate into our stories to intentionally choose a *flourishing* life.

CHAPTER 3

The Model

L IFE IS HARD enough as it is. Why would we want to further complicate our lives by spending time trying to understand a complex model that is esoteric and will never be used?

From my perspective, models are only as good as their ability to be simple, understood, and utilized. Let me give you an example of what I mean. I have worked in and with many organizations facilitating the development of comprehensive strategic plans. When I was in business school, I learned how to put together a robust strategic plan that would make your head spin. Literally. Early in my career, I would put together these multi-hundred-page strategic plans complete with graphs, tables, charts, illustrations, and projections that I thought were the greatest thing since sliced bread. I would present these plans to the senior leadership team and drop the eighty-pound (not really), professionally finished and fully bound plan in front of them and then walk out the door, nearly breaking my arm off patting myself on the back. The next time I would meet with them as part of the follow-up process, do you know what I would find? Those plans—if they were even taken out of the conference room where I emphatically dropped them in front of the senior leaders—would often have dust on them and would still creak when opened.

I was utterly confused, and to say I was disappointed did not even begin to describe how I felt inside. After experiencing this a handful of times, I knew I had two options in front of me. Option 1: Keep doing what I was doing and convince myself that my way was the correct way because that was the textbook way, and my clients needed to learn the "right" way. Option 2: Figure out what works, adjust, and provide a product that would be useful, simple to understand, and implementable. It did not take me long to figure out that if I wanted to be relevant in the world of helping leaders and organizations put together effective strategic plans, I had to change. That was a hard lesson to learn, but it was an invaluable lesson that I have carried with me to this day. I am passionate about providing simple-to-understand counsel, relevant advice, and implementable solutions to problems that are effective and impactful.

With that as context, then I ask you this: if what I present within these pages does not work, then why are you reading this? And even more importantly, why am I writing this? Too many books are written every year—too many to ever read in a lifetime. Since you have chosen to give me the gifts of your time and the money to purchase this, it is my responsibility—no, it is my duty—to provide you with a return on your investment.

I am a believer that there is "nothing new under the sun."[8] King Solomon, the author of many of the Proverbs and the book of Ecclesiastes in the Bible, is known as being the smartest and wisest man who ever lived and walked the earth. So if there is nothing new under the sun, why author this book? Why provide this model? Because I am also a believer in life experience, continu-

---

8   Eccles. 1:9 (English Standard Version).

ous improvement, and lifelong learning. Sometimes—just sometimes—learning, growth, and experience come together in such a way as to reveal something that was in front of us all along but not in a way that we understood or knew what to do with in such a way that made sense to us. With that being said, the concepts within this model are not new; however, I believe the way in which I am presenting them is.

Although I cannot necessarily promise you *revolutionary*, I can make you this promise: *transformative*. I am a pragmatist. Before I accept that something new is also great, I must know (1) Is it practical? (2) Is it relevant? (3) Does it work? In other words, is it simple to understand and use, is it relevant to my and others' lives, and does it provide the intended results? The answer to these questions as it pertains to this model is an overwhelming "YES!" So let's proceed.

The model is a triangle. Two of the strongest shapes in architecture are the triangle and the arch. I have chosen to use the triangle even though many authors have used triangles to represent their models. So why would I choose the common and often-used triangle to represent this model? Because a triangle portrays strength, growth, and movement—consistent with the concept of going on a journey as we are doing in this book. A triangle also represents the Greek letter delta, which means "change." The triangle model I present exhibits a movement upward, a change—from the base to the pinnacle.

The arrows up represent the catalysts that *accelerate* and move you toward *flourishing*. The arrows down represent the *barriers* that hinder your upward momentum that need to be overcome or mitigated to continue the journey upward to *flourishing*. The point is this: life is a journey and is something to be lived, experienced, and cherished. As we will unpack later, the reality is this: there will be times when we will experience *flourishing* in one area of our lives but not experience *flourishing* in another.

THE FLOURISHING LIFE MODEL

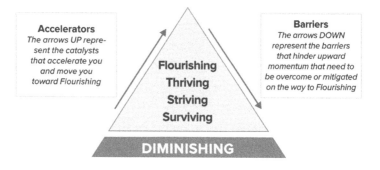

The basic premise of the model is this: *everyone can intentionally choose to pursue a flourishing life.* Regardless of one's background, education, race, religion, wealth, experience, and so forth, everyone can choose to intentionally pursue a *flourishing* life. As I mentioned earlier, the path to *flourishing* is rarely, if ever, a straight line, and it is rarely, if ever, without its challenges and setbacks. As you look at the triangle, please do not view it as a fixed shape with three sides and words inside of it. Rather, please view this triangle as a journey. If this is a journey, then we know a few facts before we even get started. What do we know about journeys? First, they have a beginning point, an ending point, and a path between those two points. Second, even the best-planned journeys are wrought with the unexpected, thereby requiring flexibility and willingness to modify the original plan. Third, most journeys will include both barriers that could prevent us from completing the journey and accelerators that could help us complete the journey. Fourth, we often learn more from the *journey* from "here" to "there" than from reaching our destination.

I will let you in on a little secret: this model, which represents a journey, is no different. Why? Because this model fits YOUR journey, which is YOUR story. Both from personal experience as well as talking with hundreds of leaders and scouring numerous books and studies, the conclusion is the same: the journey of life is where you learn, and the journey is where you experience what life is truly all about. The destinations you have in life are akin to being on an oasis in the desert, which is nearly always temporary because the journey of life calls you to something else. As you examine this model, it is easy to gravitate to the question of "What does it take to reach the pinnacle and stay there?" That is a fair question, but it is not the point of the model. The point of the model is this: *to reveal the journey*. Your life represents a journey. Along this journey, the path from *diminishing* to *flourishing*, you will encounter both accelerators and barriers. *Accelerators* are those moments, choices, relationships, and divine appointments that create opportunity and courage for change. *Barriers* are those setbacks, choices, losses, pain, hurt, and betrayals that cause us to question, doubt, and consider settling or giving up.

How about you? When was the last time you told your story? The better question is this: when was the last time you thought about your story? Your story is YOU! As we continue our journey, I will continue to ask you to think about, and eventually tell, your story.

Although everyone's journey is and will be unique, there are certain themes associated with each level of the model that provide an indicator of where you are on your journey and what you can expect to encounter on the journey to move to the next level.

In the next chapter, we will explore the definitions of each level of the model. In subsequent chapters, we will identify and define the barriers and accelerators that can help us or hinder us as we move within the model.

CHAPTER 4

Overview

NOW THAT WE have established the foundation of the model, the next few chapters will provide definition as well as structure to the model. I know definitions can be boring and tedious; however, to make sure we are on the same page, it is necessary to start by providing them for each of the layers of the model. We will start with the bottom level of *diminishing* and then move progressively up to the *flourishing* level.

To try to give you as many quick-hit data points to be able to self-evaluate where you may be on your own journey, I have put together a list of practical, relevant metrics and measurements for you to self-assess what may apply to you. Note: As you read these characteristics, please understand that not all of them will be applicable to your journey. You will have to decide what does and does not apply.

I believe that to truly experience a *flourishing* life, you must, at some point, be willing to take a deep, hard look in the mirror and evaluate yourself authentically and transparently. Socrates said,

"The unexamined life is not worth living."[9] Although I believe that life is precious and is always worth living, Socrates's point is well made. What Socrates was trying to communicate was that true health, fulfillment, and satisfaction in life comes by knowing as much about oneself—from a holistic and honest perspective—as possible.

Important Note: Before we get into the definitions of the levels, I want to address one area that affects all the levels of the model, which I considered adding to the characteristics; however, because this affects all levels of the model, I decided to address it here. The area is your *Family of Origin*. Everyone has Family of Origin issues that may need to be addressed at some point in life. Your Family of Origin issues may be minimal, and very little may need to be addressed. Perhaps your Family of Origin was healthy, and your experience gave you a functional and mature view of life. If that is the case, then your Family of Origin may serve as an *accelerator* in your story.

For some, Family of Origin issues are substantially painful and permeate every area of life. For example, if your parents are no longer together, for whatever reason, this has caused feelings of loss and possibly abandonment or rejection. If your mother is not present and especially if she has been absent for quite some time, you may not have a sense of being loved, accepted, or nurtured the way only a mother can.

If your relationship with your father is broken or nonexistent, or maybe you had an abusive or absent father growing up, this will cause a "father wound" in you that you will carry with you through your life. For context, many people have a "father wound" that has been caused by an absent, abusive, or abandoned relationship with

---

9   Plato, *Apology* (written and published circa 399–387 BCE), https://chs.harvard.edu/primary-source/plato-the-apology-of-socrates-sb/.

their dads. In my story, I refer to the "shadows I have boxed" and the "paper walls" that I have run into at times over the years. I have a substantial "father wound" that has been with me since my teenage years, and it has caused me to question my identity; it has caused an unexplained lack of confidence at times and to search, in an unhealthy way, for acceptance and approval from father "figures" throughout my life (but nothing can fill that void, except for a relationship with my Heavenly Father).

It took years of counseling and being mentored by men I loved and respected to help me address my deeply ingrained "father wound" (and it still is with me to this day, but I am much healthier and more whole). Whatever your Family of Origin story may be and whatever hurts or pains you carry with you today, please do not ignore this in your life. Without dealing with the Family of Origin issues in our lives, it is like carrying around heavy baggage with us wherever we go, and it makes life much more difficult to navigate. In addition, carrying this baggage can make it more difficult to move from one level of the Flourishing Life Model to the next.

> **How about you? What hurts, pains, or other emotional wounds and scars can you identify in your life from your Family of Origin? Make a note of these in your story because these may be significant areas of your life that you can, maybe need to, address to help you become whole and healthy.**

As you read the definitions of each level, please read the characteristics of all five levels before deciding what does or does not best describe you. Chances are that you will find yourself on one level in one area or role and on another level in another role. You may find yourself in three or even all levels as you evaluate the various roles you have. If this describes you after reading the definitions of all five, that is great. It is very plausible to be *flourishing* in one area, *thriving* in another, and *surviving* in yet another. On the other hand, I am sure some of you will find you are experiencing a *flourishing* life in most life dimensions, as I am sure there will be some of you that find you are experiencing a *diminishing* life in several (or most) life dimensions. The purpose of laying the model out this way is to provide a way for you to self-evaluate.

Part III of the book will address how you may intentionally choose to integrate the lessons from the model and make the choices to move from one level to the next. And yes, I mean intentionally because the journey of life continues onward whether we do anything intentionally or not. But to move from one level to another—especially if your heart's desire is to experience the *flourishing* life—requires an intentional mindset, an intentional choice, and an intentional modification to your journey.

Let's start with the *diminishing* level.

DEFINITIONS OF THE FIRST FOUR LEVELS OF THE MODEL

DIMINISHING

The bottom level of the model is the *diminishing* level. This is the level where hope is all but lost. Where you have tried and failed and then accepted that failure somehow just  became part of who you are. Rather than viewing the failure as an event on your journey, being on the *diminishing* level, you view failure as an integral part of your story. For whatever reason, you have lost the ability to separate failure and personhood—who you are as a person—on your journey. The *diminishing* level is where failure, hurt, disappointment, hopelessness, pain, betrayal, and sometimes despair have come to define you. The reason that I have placed the *diminishing* level as part of the triangle but a little below the triangle is because those who live at the *diminishing* level often disengage from others or do not see their inherent value or the contribution they bring to others' lives.

Characteristics of the DIMINISHING Level

- **Mindset.** "I lost." "Never try, never fail."
- **Posture/Attitude.** "I quit."
- **Relationships.** Dysfunctional, nonexistent, or codependent.
- **Work/Career.** None, or perceived to be menial or meaningless (i.e., "I hate my job").
- **Spiritual.** Believes there is no God, or if there is a God, He does not care, He is not interested, or He does not get involved.
- **Physical.** Does not care or does not try (i.e., no/little exercise; no/little commitment to healthy eating; may engage in unhealthy habits such as smoking, recreational drug use, excessive alcohol intake, binge drinking, over- or binge eating).
- **Emotional.** Sad, negative, critical, down. May experience depression, anxiety, and difficulty sleeping. Angry, maybe fits of rage.
- **Hope.** Nonexistent or lost.
- **Joy.** Nonexistent. May experience brief moments of happiness.
- **Courage.** Fear-driven. Afraid to try or make an effort because of fear of failure or letting self or others down.
- **Intellectual.** Probably not open to new experiences. May have a fixed mindset with fixed opinions. Learning based on personal experience and not from others.
- **Love.** Does not want to or may not know how to love others or self.

SURVIVING

Survival is inherent in every living creature or thing on the planet. Animals and humans are created and born with the instinct to survive. Survival in the wild for animals simply 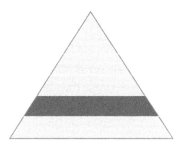 means three things: (1) food, (2) shelter, and (3) reproduction. Animals that find a way to do all three of these survive, and their species carries on. Too many humans live their existence in much the same way that animals do—searching for food, finding shelter, and seeking a mate to reproduce with. In the primitive world, there was not much more to hope for, other than companionship. Even though many, especially in affluent cultures, have access to resources beyond filling their stomachs, a roof over their heads, and someone to mate with to have kids, it seems that many choose to remain at the *surviving* level out of choice or necessity or lack of intentionally choosing a different journey. If this is true, why do so many only seem to choose *surviving* when the resources seem abundantly available to be able to pursue a *thriving* life? Because *thriving* is about so much more than available resources, but we will get to that later.

Characteristics of the SURVIVING Level

- **Mindset.** "Live and let live." Routine.
- **Posture/Attitude.** "Putting in my time." "It is what it is."
- **Relationships.** Functional. May have a close friend or two, but mostly guarded with others.
- **Work/Career.** Steady job and paycheck. May feel stuck. Not fulfilled by work. May dislike or hate the job. Work is "punching the clock."
- **Spiritual.** God may or may not exist. If God does exist, He does not care too much about me. If the individual believes

in God, they may view Him in a functional role (i.e., "If I need something, it all depends on me—God is not a 'cosmic gift-giver'").

- **Physical.** Do what is necessary to be able to live. May or may not exercise regularly. May indulge in overeating, drinking too much, or occasional recreational drug use.
- **Intellectual.** Will learn and read whatever is required to be able to function.
- **Hope.** Suppressed hope. Possibly forgotten, but not lost.
- **Joy.** Experiences joy on rare occasions. Experiences happiness from time to time.
- **Courage.** Not necessarily afraid, but not necessarily willing to take risks, even calculated ones.
- **Love.** Routine. Functional. Reliable companion. Intimate love viewed as too risky.

STRIVING

Once you get a glimpse or a taste that there is more to life than *surviving*—and you decide you want to experience more in life—the journey of *striving* has begun. Living a *striving* life is making the decision to change, to grow, to improve, to be different, to be better, and to experience something different. Making the decision to intentionally make a change and go on the journey is often the most difficult part. Remember, the journey to *flourishing* is NOT about things and stuff; it is about experiencing life, living life to its fullest, and experiencing lasting satisfaction.

Characteristics of the STRIVING Level
- **Mindset.** "I can do this!"
- **Posture/Attitude.** "If others can, so can I!" "Watch me!"
- **Relationships.** Growing. Healing. Building or rebuilding. Intentionally seeks friendships—more functional relation-

ships at first, but seeks and desires deeper connection.

- **Work/Career.** Seeks new challenges and opportunities. Seeks to grow or expand either in a current role or new role. Seeks ways to better self in current job or in new work opportunities.
- **Spiritual.** May be experiencing a spiritual awakening. Realizing or returning to the belief that God is real and actively interested and engaged in life.
- **Physical.** Adding or returning to discipline in exercise and food eating habits. Adopting a healthier lifestyle. May start addressing negative habits that could inhibit or hurt physical health (i.e., stopping smoking; not binge eating or drinking; giving up recreational drugs; other new healthy habits formed).
- **Intellectual.** Actively seeks reading of books. May listen to podcasts or other forms of intellectual stimulations. May seek conversations that stimulate, expand, and challenge thinking.
- **Emotional.** Stable and excited about new learning, growth, and opportunities. May experience highs and lows.
- **Hope.** In the process of being restored and growing.
- **Joy.** Growing in both intensity and frequency.
- **Courage.** Fearful at times but moving forward despite it. Growing stronger every day.
- **Love.** Growing. Healing and mending. Excitement and spark return—infrequently at first, but growing in both intensity and in frequency.

THRIVING

What does it mean to thrive? As we explored in the opening pages, the standard definition of *thriving* is to accumulate and grow in wealth,

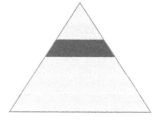

possessions, or material things. It is difficult to define *thriving* specifically and definitively. Why? Because each person is different and therefore may experience *thriving* at different thresholds or by using different criteria. It is fair to define the typical characteristics of what it means to thrive or what one experiences when *thriving* to give a high-level benchmark of what *thriving* may look like for you. *Thriving* is feeling like you are not only effective in a particular role or function, but you are also good at it, and others see and say the same.

Characteristics of the THRIVING Level

- **Mindset.** "I am on top of the world!"
- **Posture/Attitude.** "I can do whatever I set my mind to doing."
- **Relationships.** Mutually beneficial relationships. Actively seeks relationships.
- **Work/Career.** Dialed in. Viewed as a leader or a subject matter expert. Highly proficient in role. Usually "all-in" and may struggle with workaholism or making work a higher priority than other areas of life. Often lives to work (versus works to live).
- **Spiritual.** Actively growing relationship with God in prayer. Regular scripture reading. Committed to a church and serves in some capacity. May be part of a small group.
- **Physical.** Good discipline of regular exercise. Healthy eating and lifestyle habits. May overindulge from time to time, but not engaged in detrimental habits.
- **Intellectual.** Actively learns and grows to increase skills and proficiencies. Actively seeks engaging and stimulating conversations. Seeks new knowledge and learning.
- **Emotional.** Well-balanced. Excited and passionate about life. Seeks new experiences.
- **Hope.** Rooted in past track record of success. Confident of future successes.

- **Joy.** May experience joy on a regular basis. Happiness experienced often because of being associated closely with having experienced success and having the ability to afford certain luxuries and experiences.
- **Courage.** Expressed out of past success from taking risks that resulted in success. Future risk-taking calculated on a risk-reward basis. The greater the opportunity for reward, the more likely the courage to take risk.
- **Love.** Experienced out of a heart of mutual reward and benefit. Sacrificial love given at times, but if sacrifice becomes the norm, the love may fade.

That wraps up the first four levels of the Flourishing Life Model. I purposely wanted to take a break between the first four levels and the final level, *flourishing.* I just threw a lot at you, and I want to encourage you to take a moment to let the first four levels soak in before proceeding to the final level of the model. In the next chapter, our journey moves to the *flourishing* level of the model. I will intentionally be spending more time defining *flourishing* for you than the other levels of the model because this is a new way of thinking about *flourishing,* and therefore, it needs the proper amount of time to unpack and define.

The distinction between *thriving* and *flourishing* can be confusing because, on its surface, *thriving* seems like a good life to have, and for some, it is! If you desire *more* and *better* and want to focus on accumulation, then please pursue a *thriving* life for as long as that brings you satisfaction and purpose. If or when you reach a point where the pursuit of *thriving* by pursuing *more* and *better* leads to unsatisfaction and lack of purpose in your life, please consider the pursuit of *flourishing* as a viable alternative for your quest for satisfaction, meaning, and purpose in your life. After you have contemplated the first four levels of the model, please continue your journey into the next chapter, where our path will take us on a visit with *flourishing.*

CHAPTER 5

DEFINITIONS

The Final Level of the Model

FLOURISHING

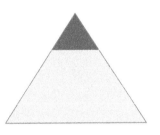

The pinnacle of the model. The top. The peak. But what does it truly mean to live a *flourishing* life? One could think that only the best of the best reaches the top of the heap—the most talented of the talented, the smartest of the smart, the GOAT (greatest of all time) in all areas of life. It is easy to assume that the best of the best are the only ones who experience a *flourishing* life. Although some may make the argument that this is *flourishing*, I do not agree with that assumption, and I am not here to make that argument whatsoever. In fact, I would like to present a completely different point of view on what the *flourishing* life is all about. *Flourishing*—or experiencing a *flourishing* life—is not something reserved only for the elite, the greatest of all time, the privileged, or whatever label you want to attach to this. It is quite the opposite. I surmise that the majority—perhaps the vast majority—of those who our society and culture say have reached the pinnacle of life and have the life that everyone envies, are experiencing a *thriving* life but not a *flourishing* life.

So, then, what does it mean to live a *flourishing* life? I quoted Eric Liddell, one of my lifelong heroes, in the beginning pages of this book. Liddell said, *"God made me to run and to run fast. When I run, I feel God's pleasure!"*[10]

How about you? When was the last time you felt or knew you were fulfilled? When was the last time you felt fully and completely satisfied? If you are a God person like Eric Liddell—like me—when was the last time you "felt God's pleasure"?

Think about that. Pray about that. Ask others when they observed that in you. Make a list. Ask your spouse, your kids, your boss, your colleagues, your direct reports, your best friend, your small group, or your pastor. When have they seen you *flourish*?

How about you? When have you known, "Wow, that was what I was created to be and to do"? When did you know that what you were doing fulfilled you, made you feel complete, and fit you? Once you have your list, you are ready to move on. Even if your list is only one thing, that is okay.

---

10   *Chariots of Fire* (Enigma Productions, 1981).

Flourishing is *more* than, but it is also *less* than. We live in a culture that says, "Just Do It,"[11] "Have It Your Way,"[12] and "Experience More." But what does all this mean? We see the commercials on television. We see the ads in magazines, online, and on billboards. All these messages seem to portray the life we "should" have, "want" to have, or "need" to have. My question is, *Really?* Would I be fulfilled drinking cold beer on a beach with scantily clad women all day long? Would I be fulfilled wearing a watch that costs tens of thousands of dollars or driving a car that costs multiple years of my salary? Would having a second home on a lake, at a ski resort, or next to the ocean truly bring me *satisfaction?* Is this the measure of true success? Will having any of this tell me *I have arrived?* Some would say yes. If this describes you and you would say yes to this, then to you I say, "Go for it—pursue your heart's desire!" For others, including myself, that answer is an unequivocal no!

I have experienced success in life. I signed my document as "president" of a company when I was twenty-three years old. I have traveled to over forty countries. I have been part of the senior executive team in several organizations. I have been to exclusive events, driven fast and luxurious cars, stayed in mansions and castles, had designer clothes, and have both seen and experienced much of what society says is living life and living it to the fullest. Was it cool? Yes. Did it bring me happiness? Only for a moment. Did it bring me fulfillment, joy, and satisfaction? NO!

I heard an illustration once by a speaker, and I wish I knew who shared it because I would love to thank the person—it made a profound impact on me. The illustration was this:

So many people spend their lives climbing the corporate

---

11 Nike Slogan, coined in 1988.
12 Burger King Slogan, coined in 1974.

ladder (and that can be in business, nonprofit, church, academia, public service). They climb over and use people and make choices, decisions, and sacrifices every time they take a step up the ladder—sometimes even choosing to violate their convictions, beliefs, and morals. When they have finally reached the top of the ladder, often they make a startling discovery. The ladder is either leaning against the wrong wall, or there is another, higher, more-attractive-looking ladder, or the view from the top was nothing like what they hoped or imagined.

I heard this illustration many years ago, and since then, I have heard story after story, and I know people personally who told me that this was exactly what happened to them. So why do we continue to do this—why do we continue to climb the ladder? For some, it is because it is all they know. For others, they feel like they do not have a choice. And yet for others, they feel like they are not doing it for themselves but for their loved ones and for other more altruistic reasons. And still, for others, they do it intentionally because that is what they genuinely want to do.

How about you? Where are you in this story?

If you are in the last category and you are *flourishing* in doing this, then please keep doing that! For everyone else, I have one simple question for you: Why? Why are you still climbing the ladder when you know—not directly, but you know it intuitively in your gut—that the top of the ladder is not really what you want? I am happy to say that there is another way.

For some, climbing the corporate ladder is exactly what you are called to do. If that is what you are called and equipped to do, you are good at doing it, and you are passionate about doing that, then do it. We need gifted, experienced, and driven C-suite executives who are called and equipped to lead government, academia, business, nonprofits, NGOs, and the arts. And, please, do it with all of you and with excellence in all you do. To do anything else will be less than fulfilling for you and will not bring you joy. In other words, you will not experience the *flourishing* life if you pursue anything other than what you are equipped, experienced, gifted, and passionate about doing. And if you do pursue that, please make sure that you do it in such a way that you and others are inspired to live a *flourishing* life that causes others to want to do the same.

I have spent thirty-two years of my life climbing, clawing, scratching my way to the top of the ladders I was climbing, and do you know what I discovered? There is always, *always* a bigger ladder, or a ladder with a bigger and better view, or the view from the top of the ladder is nothing like you imagined. If money, power, wealth, status, and prestige are the answer to a fulfilled, joyful, and satisfied life, why do we keep seeing example after example of these same people searching for more? Because there is a vast difference between living a *thriving* life and living a *flourishing* life.

I am not knocking or picking on those who are blessed with riches, talent, and wealth beyond what most of us will ever experience or have in this life. I am simply offering an explanation and a perspective as to why riches, power, wealth, prestige, or elitism are not enough. These things all fall in the *thriving* bucket. Our culture—Western culture, in particular—says that these things are the answer to a fulfilling, joyful, and satisfied life. Do you want to know a little secret? They are not! I have been in developing countries with families with thatch roofs, dirt floors, and kids with no shoes, who are truly more fulfilled, joyful, and satisfied than most—and I mean *most*—of the families and kids that I know in Europe and the United States. Why? That is the focus and the purpose of this book.

A life that flourishes is a life that pours out—a life that gives back. A *flourishing* life is a life that lives beyond oneself. A *flourishing* life focuses and thinks beyond this life. A *flourishing* life is a life that is more concerned with legacy, impact, and giving back than with getting, accumulating, and growing in fame and fortune. The *flourishing* life is more concerned with impact and influence over power and prestige. The *flourishing* life is more concerned with giving over getting. The *flourishing* life is more concerned with sacrifice over comfort. The *flourishing* life is more concerned with contributing over consuming. The *flourishing* life is more concerned with experiences over things. The *flourishing* life is more concerned with legacy over temporal. And the *flourishing* life is more concerned with story over *CliffsNotes*. From a spiritual perspective, a *flourishing* life is more concerned with building God's kingdom over building one's own personal empire.

Summarized, *flourishing* is living a life dedicated to something that is beyond you—it is living a surrendered life to your calling (or to God's calling for you, if you prefer). As I mentioned earlier, *flourishing* is living at the intersection of your passion, what you are gifted and skilled at doing, what has been confirmed and affirmed by others, and your calling.

Characteristics of the FLOURISHING Level

- **Mindset.** "I am fulfilled—truly fulfilled—and satisfied when I live my dreams and out of my true calling."
- **Posture/Attitude.** "How can I best contribute and invest in you today?"
- **Relationships.** Has and actively pursues relationships that are "iron sharpening iron" (Proverbs 27:17)—where each makes the other person better. Seeks to give to others out of a heart of gratefulness and generosity. Wants the best for others. Spurs others to be the best version of who they are and can become.

- **Work/Career.** Keeps work and job in its proper perspective (contrasted with the *thriving* level where work tends to become one's life). Works to live versus lives to work.
- **Spiritual.** Believes in God. Has an active, personal, and growing relationship with God. Actively engaged in a church. Pursues living a surrendered life to God and to His will. Explanation: A "surrendered" life can, on its face and without definition, appear to be negative—as in an abandoned life or a life where someone has quit or given up. A surrendered life is exactly the opposite of this. A surrendered life is one that lives beyond oneself. A surrendered life lives for God, for others, for a calling, a vision, a mission, or a dream that is bigger than oneself. Living a "surrendered life" means intentionally putting others' needs above your own, and it means being open to whatever and wherever God may choose to lead or use you—in the small things and the big things.
- **Physical.** Seeks healthy balance—meaning a healthy life rhythm of balance of exercise, meal planning, sleep, rest, time off, work, play, and family.
- **Intellectual.** Committed to lifelong learning and growth. Seeks intellectual challenges. Seeks understanding of others' opinions and viewpoints—even those different from one's own. Knows what you believe and why you believe it; however, you hold your opinions loosely and seek truth and reality above opinion, fictional truth, or an invented narrative.
- **Emotional.** Experiences stability and is considered to be a bedrock. A safe place for others to vent, let down their hair, and be oneself. Nonjudgmental. Open to others, which is why people who are struggling or hurting will seek you out. Genuine, transparent, and authentic. Without pretense.
- **Hope.** Hope-filled and hope-ful. Acknowledges and embraces that hope does not come from within you—it

comes from knowing that this life is but a vapor and so short. Embraces this life as a time of character development and a time to invest in what really matters—people, relationships, influence, giving and generosity, pouring out and investing of oneself into others.

- Joy. Joy-filled. Explanation: Joy is not happiness—it is so much more. Happiness is temporary and is rooted in what you are experiencing right now. There are moments of extreme happiness in life: a newborn; baby's first steps; getting the first hit in baseball; scoring that first basket or goal; your first date; your first kiss; graduation day; wedding day; your first job; your first car; your first promotion; and the list goes on. All of these are amazing experiences! But what happens when the date ends? The game is over? Today turns into tomorrow. We all need to experience happiness and these happy moments in life, but there must be more that sustains us from one happy moment to the next. Because in between happy, there is also sad, loss, pain, and hurt, but even in those moments, we can experience fulfillment, joy, and satisfaction. How? By understanding where joy comes from. Joy is not based on what we do or experience—it is based on who we are, or more importantly, who God says we are. Joy is rooted in identity. No matter what you experience in life—the good and the bad, the highs and the lows, the victory and the defeat, the wins and the losses—you always know who you are. You always know that *you* are a child of God, regardless of what the world tries to tell you or regardless of what you experience.

How about you? Where is your source of joy? What is your source of identity?

- **Courage.** The *flourishing* life is a courageous life. The *flourishing* life understands the risks and understands the fears but chooses to move forward despite those fears. I am not talking about some reckless, daredevil approach to life. I am talking about taking calculated risks. I am talking about understanding the fears we all face and still making the intelligent choice to not be held captive by our fears. Fear is a liar. Fear keeps us from experiencing life to the fullest. For example, for years, I was afraid of flying because I was not in control! When I had my family business, there were annual incentives to increase revenue given by certain suppliers. The business was growing year over year, and for several years in a row, my business won all-expense-paid trips to some amazing places. The first year, it was the US Virgin Islands. I gave it away. The second year, it was Hawai'i. I gave that trip to my mom. The third year was Banff National Park. I gave it away, and then it hit me. Why was I doing this? Why was I not experiencing these things? I tried to convince myself it was because I was benevolent and wanted to reward others. The truth was this: *I was scared.* I was afraid of flying, and I was convinced I was going to die in a plane crash. At peak operational times, there are over 5,400 aircraft in the sky.[13] I was convinced the plane I was on was going to crash. So I did not fly. After I gave up my trip to Banff—a place on my bucket list—I made the decision that I would never pass up the opportunity to travel by air again, especially to places on my bucket list. Since then, I have flown over three million miles to over forty different countries. I would have missed these

---

[13]   "Air Traffic by the Numbers," Federal Aviation Administration, last modified June 15, 2022, https://www.faa.gov/air_traffic/by_the_numbers/

amazing cultures, people, and experiences had I chosen to stay captured by my fear of flying. I am not saying I am a courageous person, but this is an example of how not having courage can keep us from experiencing life to the fullest—a *flourishing* life.

How about you? What fear is keeping you from experiencing life to the fullest, a *flourishing* life?

- Love. "Greater love has no one than this, that someone lay down his life for his friends."[14] The *flourishing* life experiences love out of a heart of loving someone else despite who they are. The most selfless kind of love that anyone can experience is when someone intentionally sacrifices their life for the life of someone else. This is what Jesus did for all of humanity. Why? Because Jesus understood true love. Love can be such a difficult, ethereal concept to grasp and understand. It is beyond the scope of this book—and way out of my pay grade—to try to define "love" or convince you that I have somehow found the formula to true love. What I offer, instead, is this: the *flourishing* life loves and loves deeply, selflessly, and sacrificially. The *flourishing* life understands that true love means loving without expecting anything in return. True love means giving without getting. True love means loving without the expectation of being loved in return.

That sums up the high-level characteristics of each level of the

---

14   John 15:13 (English Standard Version).

model. I spent more time explaining the *flourishing* characteristics, but a deeper and more thorough explanation was necessary for *flourishing* for two reasons. First, to help unpack what I mean by *flourishing*. The second reason is to better compare and contrast *flourishing* with *thriving*.

Why is it important to provide this kind of differentiation? As I mentioned previously, on the surface, it can appear as though pursuing a *thriving* life is just as good as (or even better than, depending on your perspective) pursuing a *flourishing* life. If this describes you, then wonderful, please pursue whatever level appeals to you the most. You need to decide for yourself which level most describes your life currently and which level most appeals to where you would like to move to in your journey. And that means for some, reaching the *thriving* level of life is good for you. If this describes you, I am truly happy for you! As I mentioned before, if you ever reach a point where *thriving* no longer brings you satisfaction and meaning, please consider pursuing a *flourishing* life as a viable alternative to finding meaning and purpose for your life. The bottom line is this: It is more important that you make the decision to live an intentional life, not an accidental or unintentional one. So whatever level you choose to pursue—if it is your intentional choice—then pursue your journey full-on and all-in.

How about you? Now that we have journeyed through the characteristics of each level of the model, which level do you most identify with? Which level or levels would you like to grow in and pursue in your life's journey?

As a reminder, we will be identifying specific exercises in Part III where you will have the opportunity to dive deep into the concepts of the model and apply them specifically to your life.

The next chapter will examine *accelerators* and *barriers* to each level of the model.

CHAPTER 6

Accelerators and Barriers

HAVE YOU EVER wanted to do something, and for whatever reason, it seemed like it just wasn't happening for you, no matter what you tried? Conversely, have you ever tried to do something, and it seemed like it went so much smoother and easier than you ever thought possible? This, at a high level, is what it is like when you experience *barriers* or *accelerators* in your life. *Barriers* can prevent you from doing the things you really want to do, and *accelerators* can help propel you to be able to do what you really want to do.

As you have undoubtedly experienced *barriers* and *accelerators* to what you want to do from time to time in your life, the Flourishing Life Model has natural *accelerators* and *barriers* that accompany each level. We will be unpacking those characteristics that serve as *accelerators*—that which helps propel us on our journey to the next level—and those that serve as *barriers*—that which can prevent us or slow us down on our journey to the next level.

Important Note: The list of *accelerators* and *barriers* for each of the levels I am presenting is in no way an exhaustive list. The characteristics chosen for each are meant to serve as examples and as catalysts for your thinking and self-evaluation as you process and evaluate their application to your life. As in the prior chapter, where we examined the characteristics of each level, I ask you to self-evaluate as you read. Which of these *accelerators* and *barriers* do you see inherent in your life? If you identify an *accelerator*, how will you leverage that to help propel your journey forward? If you identify a *barrier*, what do you need to work on or seek help with to overcome or mitigate the *barrier* so it doesn't slow you down or prevent you on your journey? As before, please read all the *accelerators* and all the *barriers* before deciding what may or may not be true for you. As with the characteristics we evaluated for each level, these are fluid—meaning what may currently be an *accelerator* or *barrier* may not have been at a different stage of life or may not be in a future stage of life. Life is dynamic, and as a result, we experience life differently as we grow older and, hopefully, wiser.

ACCELERATORS AND BARRIERS TO DIMINISHING

ACCELERATORS in the DIMINISHING level

What can help propel you from *Diminishing* to the next level, *Surviving*?

- **Making the intentional decision to try again.** Making the decision to cast aside your fears, your past failures, or your past experiences and try again. Making the decision to take one step and then take another step. This is you deciding that you are moving from the *diminishing* level to the next level up.

- **Believing there is more/better/healthier and believing you can have it.** Moving from *diminishing* starts with a belief—a belief that you do not have to accept defeat, your current state, or your destiny. Life throws hard punches, but you can punch back. It starts with believing! Without belief, there is no way out or up. Sometimes believing there is something better does not start with you; it starts with someone else believing in you.
- **Hope.** Hope is a powerful force—emotionally and intellectually. Hope kept Jews alive who were imprisoned, tortured, and starving in concentration camps until they were liberated during World War II. Hope kept prisoners of war alive until they were freed, even though they were locked in cells without food and water, with rats and stifling heat. Hope keeps a vision and a dream alive when everyone around us abandons us. Hope. Hope gives a belief that our lives can experience more.
- **Love.** Love is more powerful than hope. Moving from *diminishing* usually requires something that motivates you to move, and nothing is more powerful to experience than love. Sometimes that means being loved by someone else; sometimes that means realizing that every one of us—regardless of age, gender, race, religion, or creed—is loved by someone. Sometimes that love is flesh and blood. Sometimes it is coming face to face with our mortality and realizing there is someone who loves us even if we do not love ourselves. This was the love that I experienced when I was in the depths of despair in my early twenties. I experienced this love from my wife, my mom, my maternal grandparents, my pastor, and Jesus. Without others loving me and without realizing that my identity is who Jesus says I am, I may have stayed at the *diminishing* level. But by grace and love, I was given a different vision of not only who I was, but who I could be.

How about you? Who loves you—just the way you are?

In the continued spirit of sharing my heart and what is important to me—not to proselytize or try to convince you of anything—if you cannot answer this with anyone who is flesh and blood, there is another, and His name is the Name above All Names. Jesus loves you. Sounds so cliché, doesn't it? Many of us learned the song when we were just wee little, but oh, how true and real this song became for me as I reached my forties. "Jesus loves me, this I know."[15] Guess what? He loves you too. And He loves you if you believe it or choose not to believe it. And sometimes, that is all we need to know.

BARRIERS in the DIMINISHING level

What can keep you from moving from *Diminishing* toward the next level, *Surviving*?

- **Having a victim mindset.** In other words, choosing to blame others, choosing to have pity on yourself, choosing to make excuses for where you are in life.
- **Captured and imprisoned by fear.** Allowing fear to keep you from acting.
- **Choosing to give up and not try again.** If you are at the point where you just do not have the energy or desire to try again, you have run into a *barrier* at the *diminishing* level.
- **Feeling alone.** Feeling that no one cares or that you have no value or do not matter.

---

15   L.O. Emerson, "Jesus Loves Me," (Boston: Oliver Ditson & Company, 1873), Library of Congress.

- **Believing the lie that this is all there is.** The biggest and most common barrier to the diminishing person is believing the lie that this is all there is and there is nothing else.
- **Told repeatedly that this is all you will amount to in life, or this is what you deserve.** The most powerful force in the world is not wind, water, or fire—it is the tongue. In the book of James in the New Testament of the Bible, James (one of the brothers of Jesus) addresses the power of the tongue.[16] The tongue has the power to give life and take it away. Nothing will breathe life into a person like the power of words, and nothing takes life away from a person like the power of words. When I was a kid, I used to say what every kid says at some point, "Sticks and stones will break my bones, but words will never hurt me!" It was not until I was into my twenties that I realized how big of a lie that childhood saying really was. There have been times in my life when I would have much preferred to have been hit with a stick or a stone than dealing with the hurtful words from someone who I thought cared about and loved me.
- **Giving up.** Stop trying. Stop living. Believing it just is not worth it anymore. The diminished person lives a *diminishing* life. Life is hard, and life can be downright brutal at times. **Life is not measured by how many times we get knocked down but by how many times we get back up.** For some, life deals a near-fatal blow. The saddest and most excruciating story in life is the one where someone chooses to stop living, but they are still physically alive, or when a person is knocked down and they decide not to get back up. A life that checks out but still draws breath is a life that is a *diminishing* life. But there is so much more. There is hope;

---

16   James 3:1–12 (English Standard Version).

if there is hope, there is life—at least there is the promise of life.

ACCELERATORS AND BARRIERS TO SURVIVING

ACCELERATORS in the SURVIVING level

What can help propel you from *Surviving* to the next level, *Striving*?

What are the *accelerators* to moving from *surviving* to *striving*? Without using clichés or simple formulaic answers, *accelerators* to move from *surviving* to *striving* usually mean that something must break—life must stop working. Otherwise, it is too easy to stay at the *surviving* level without a catalyst that makes you realize that something just is not working in your life.

- **Hope.** I know I used hope before, but hope is such a powerful positive motivator. Hope gives us all a glimpse of something greater than our current reality.
- **Growth in self-awareness.** What does it mean to grow in self-awareness? It means growing in your understanding of who you are—your strengths, your weaknesses, your gifts, your abilities, your limitations, your experiences. Growing in self-awareness means accepting reality and growing in the knowledge of who you truly are—your identity. Reading this book will help you grow in self-awareness. Completing the exercises in Part III of this book will *really* help you grow in self-awareness.
- **Life stops working.** When what you have always done stops working, then what is next? How do you make your life start working again? One option is to figure out how to start *surviving* again. The problem is that this rarely works. Why? Because everything that made life work before, once it breaks, scares you to the point you realize two things: (1)

there is no going back, and (2) building what it will take to go back to *surviving* again is just too stinking hard. So you start to search for more. You start *striving*.

- **Someone loves you enough to show you another way.** When life broke for me, I had a beloved friend take the risk of telling me that there was another way—I did not have to live a *surviving* life any longer. My life stopped working, and my friend not only painted a picture of a different life for me but also walked with me during the transition from *surviving* to *striving*. I will explain more details of this in Part II when I share my story.

> **How about you? Do you have a friend who loves you and is or has been telling you there is another way to live, that you do not have to live like you have been living?**

- **The courage to change.** Every move, every change, and every decision requires courage. The courage to move beyond *surviving*. Because *surviving* is predictable, it is known, it is comfortable, and it can be difficult to move beyond *surviving*. Sometimes all it takes is a taste—a taste that there is something more than just living from sunrise to sunset. This has nothing to do with possessions, money, lush vacations, or second houses. This has everything to do with experiencing a life that is beyond *surviving*.

BARRIERS to SURVIVING

What can keep you from moving from *Surviving* toward the next level, *Striving*?

Living a *surviving* life can become your identity. I know. I lived this way for much of my adult life, and I wore it with honor and pride. But guess what happened? Life happened. Life broke. And with that, my identity of being a *survivor* also broke. For me, it was not a moment or a bright and shining revelation. It was a progressive realization that my life just was not working any longer. For me, *surviving* got me through the first half of my life (Lord willing, I am only at the halfway point!), but it was not going to get me through the next half, or the next twenty-five years, or the next five years, or the next one year. So what kept me from moving up sooner? *Barriers.*

- **Believing this is the best there is.** If you have come to believe that *surviving* is the best there is for you, you have run into a *barrier.* The truth is this: there is so much more for you in life, and there is so much more for you to experience.

NOTE: My use of *more* in these bullet points is not the same *more* as accumulation of *more* money, power, possessions, title, or position that I referenced earlier in the book. The use of more in these bullets relates to more health, more balance, more purpose, more meaning, more satisfaction, more fulfillment, and more joy.

- **It works.** *Surviving* works. *Surviving* is known. It becomes comfortable. Having something that is known can be so much easier and comfortable than the unknown. *Surviving* can work, and it can work for a long time—sometimes for a lifetime. *Surviving* works, until it doesn't. Then what? Then, either you search for more, or you move down to *diminishing* and give up. I contemplated both—trust me, I did—but decided there had to be more.
- **Surviving becomes an identity.** *Surviving* can be a defining identity. It was for me. I was a survivor, and I was proud of

it. Those who knew me or knew of me also knew it, and they wondered how. How was I able to survive in the face of adversity? I wore the label of "survivor" with enormous pride. It became my identity. It also became my idol and my downfall.

- **Surviving is predictable.** When *surviving* is your identity and it works, it is also predictable. *Surviving* becomes predictable because you know what it requires of you to survive: you must struggle, fight, and win. Period. That is *surviving*. Nothing more and nothing less. To survive means to outlast. To be the last person standing. To play the game better than the rest. It does not mean you have to be the best—you just must be better than your competitor. The problem? It is exhausting. It is an exhausting existence. Not only do you have to constantly fight your known competitors, but you must fight your unknown ones as well. I spent more time and energy boxing shadows than I ever did boxing real competitors. And that is the fundamental problem with living the *surviving* life.

ACCELERATORS AND BARRIERS TO STRIVING

ACCELERATORS in the STRIVING level

What can help propel you from *striving* to the next level, *Thriving*?

- **New or renewed belief.** When life breaks, a vision or dream is often lost as well, or a loss of a dream may cause your life to break. Moving from *striving* to *thriving* often means that a new, or renewed, belief or vision has emerged that motivates you to keep moving.
- **Deciding enough is enough.** Making the decision that what is current reality is no longer acceptable is a common

theme throughout this book. Why? Because we all have a choice to make: be the victim or be empowered and then intentionally decide to start moving. Deciding not to move backward and deciding that you can choose a step forward. Decide to start and to keep moving—enough is enough!

- **Realize problems are opportunities, not problems.** Too many times, problems can derail us, and most of the time, those problems present us with opportunities to gain experience, grow, learn, improve, and get better. Reframe the problem to be solved into an opportunity to gain experience and grow.

- **Eliminating paper walls.** What are paper walls? Paper walls are walls, barriers, and limitations that exist only in our mind. They do not actually exist. The difference between moving up to *thriving* or back to *surviving* is realizing that paper walls are not real.

How about you? What are the paper walls in your life that are threatening to keep you from moving forward?

The reality is, we all must deal with paper walls; however, the issue is how we respond to them. Make the decision to run through your paper walls!

BARRIERS in the STRIVING level

What can keep you from moving from *Striving* toward the next level, *Thriving*?

- **Lack of confidence.** Even though you get a taste of a life that is more than *surviving*, you start to wonder, "Can this really be something for me? Can I do this?" The answer is always yes. And the answer is always no. How can it be both yes and no? At some point on our journey, we get to a crucial inflection point—the proverbial fork in the road. The point where we must choose the common road or the road less traveled. Robert Frost famously said, "Two roads diverged in a wood and I—I took the one less traveled by, and that has made all the difference."[17] At some point, we all get to make a choice: the road commonly chosen or the one less traveled.

How about you? What road will you choose?

The one less traveled requires courage and confidence. Not the *I will succeed* kind of confidence but the kind of confidence that says, "I am all-in, I have 'burned my ships,' and I am not looking back, no matter what!" Which road will you choose?

- **Keeping options open.** I used this illustration earlier, but it works well to make this point. In 1519, Hernán Cortés arrived in the New World with 600 men.[18] After all the men had disembarked on the new land, Cortés had the ships burned, effectively sealing the fate of all 600 men—there was no turning back. Two years later, Cortés and his men defeated the Aztec Empire and established their rule in the

---

17   Robert Frost, *The Road Not Taken: A Selection of Robert Frost's Poems* (New York: Henry Holt and Company, 1991).
18   Winston A. Reynolds, "The Burning Ships of Hernán Cortés," *Hispania* 42, no 3 (September 1959): 317–24, https://doi.org/10.2307/335707.

New World. History often speculated what would have happened had the ships not been burned: Would they have turned back? Would the Aztecs have defeated them? Those questions are forever lost to history because the reality is this: they burned their ships. As a result, we have the history we know: Cortés and his men conquered the Aztecs. In using this example, I am not condoning what Cortés and his men did to the Aztecs. Rather, the purpose for using this illustration is the commitment these men were forced to make when all options were removed from them after their ships were burned.

> **How about you? What ship or ships do you need to burn? What options are you keeping open that could give you the opportunity to retreat or move back to the known and the comfort of *surviving*? What options do you need to eliminate to move forward and not backward?**

- Concentration of effort. In other words, focus. To have the greatest opportunity to thrive (i.e., move to the next level), you must make the decision to focus. Pick an area, a topic, a passion, a skillset, a dream—something that you can be all-in about—and do that. The key to accomplishment and success is the concentration of effort. It has been said that to become an expert in something, it takes 10,000 hours of practice.[19] At forty hours per week for fifty-two weeks per

---

19   Malcolm Gladwell, *Outliers: The Story of Success* (New York: Little, Brown and Company, 2008).

year, that is a minimum of five years, and that assumes you are committed to it for eight hours per day for five days per week, every week of the year for five years. But here is the problem: *who does that?* We live in a world full of distractions. We have a supercomputer attached to our hands (i.e., our phones), in our pockets, in our purses, or otherwise accessible to us 24/7, 365. Although having a smartphone that connects us to the world in an instant can be a wonderful asset and blessing, it is also extremely distracting. I am convinced that your smartphone keeps you wonderfully connected, and it keeps you terribly isolated at the same time. It keeps you informed, and it keeps you uninformed because you miss what is going on right in front of you in real time. It allows you to be accessible and effective, and it keeps you tethered and ineffective. It allows you to be good at what you have done, and it keeps you from being great at what you are passionate about doing and becoming.

ACCELERATORS AND BARRIERS TO THRIVING

ACCELERATORS in the THRIVING level

What can help propel you from *Thriving* toward the next level, *Flourishing?*

- **Being unsatisfied and feeling discontented.** The longing for something else—when you already have what you want—which has nothing to do with wanting more. It has to do with having much but not being satisfied or not feeling fulfilled with what you already have. It is realizing that more—more money, more power, more things, more prestige—is not the answer. When you have achieved and reached the pinnacle—and you are *thriving*, and it is not enough, then what? Remember earlier when I used the ladder example? When you have climbed every ladder of success that you can fathom and it seems like you reach the top of the ladder only to discover that the view has not changed, or worse yet, there is a higher ladder and then a higher ladder after that, then what? Many people spend their entire professional lives climbing ladders because they think there is a higher and better ladder, only to discover that at the top of the next ladder, the view just isn't that much different, and there always seems to be another ladder that is higher and more appealing. If this describes your journey, you may just be searching for something more than *thriving*. Your journey toward *flourishing* may be beginning.

- **An awakening within you.** Making the jump from *thriving* to *flourishing* often requires a catalyst that triggers an internal chain reaction that leads to the pursuit of greater purpose and fulfillment that is absent in the *thriving* life. Many times, a person will either begin or continue a spiritual journey. The premise for this journey is often rooted in a growing recognition that there is something in life that is bigger than oneself. We will explore more of this in the next section, but the move from *thriving* to *flourishing* is a move from inward to outward, from getting to giving, from pouring in to pouring out, from accumulating to distributing. It is exceedingly difficult to move from *thriving* to *flourishing* without first realizing that there is something so much bigger than you (and me) in life. Consistent with my story throughout this book, for me, it was coming to the realization that Jesus Christ is exactly who He said He was. With that dawning realization, it caused a crisis of belief in me that led to my surrendering my life to Him and to His will. Through this relationship, I began to realize that there is so much more to life than pursuing wealth, fortune, power, and position. The older I have gotten, the more I have been unable to escape the overwhelming draw of a life fully committed to what God has called me to, and not drawn to a life that is committed to whatever I want it to be.

- **A shift of focus.** *Thriving* often focuses on here and now with little thought to tomorrow, especially in the context of legacy. Shifting focus from now to the future and emphasizing legacy over current reputation is a definitive indicator of moving from *thriving* to *flourishing*. Shifting to legacy thinking is shifting focus to the end of one's life and looking back at one's life. As you look back over your life, a legacy focus is a focus on influence, relationships, and impact that outlives our lives. When I was a youth pastor, I would do an exercise every year where I would have each student write his or her eulogy, focusing on what they would most want to have said about them at their own funeral by those who loved them the most. We will unpack this more in Part III of the book. For now, if you identify with the *thriving* stage and you feel as though your focus is beginning to shift to something bigger than you and longer term, your journey may be approaching the *flourishing* level.

BARRIERS in the THRIVING level

What can keep you from moving from *Thriving* toward the next level, *Flourishing*?

- **Thriving is a good life.** When you are *thriving*, why would you want to reach for more? There cannot be more, can there? I am making good money, I have a good life, and I have worked hard for this. If *flourishing* means I must give up the life I have worked so hard to get, why would I want to do that? The *thriving* life is a good life, and for some, that will be good enough. If that describes you, wonderful! Please continue to live your best life. For others, *thriving* will be a good life, but questions have begun to creep into your life that make you wonder if there is a greater purpose and meaning to life.

- **Having a happy and enviable life.** One of the biggest challenges with moving from *thriving* to *flourishing* is that *thriving* often leads to a level of life experience that is enviable. Remember, the definition of *thriving* is to accumulate and gain. It is obvious that a *thriving* life has opportunities and benefits that become difficult to imagine living without. There are many upsides to the *thriving* life; however, there are many downsides as well. "I am happy" quickly becomes "I am bored." "This is new and exciting" becomes "This is old and stale." The latest and greatest becomes quickly outdated, worn out, yesterday's news, or last year's model. I have experienced, witnessed, read about, and seen firsthand the destruction and the devastation that can happen when boredom, unrest, impatience, and a lack of contentment take hold of a person's psyche. Marriages are blown apart by affairs. Businesses are bankrupted due to overspending. Mountains of debt are accumulated due to out-of-control spending. Reputations are dashed due to compromising one's values and beliefs. My question is this: Why? Why does this happen? If *thriving* is the pinnacle we are to aspire to in life and then it is achieved, why does it not produce long-lasting satisfaction, happiness, and fulfillment? I am convinced it is because *thriving* is not the ultimate destination. *Thriving* may lead to *happiness*, which is temporary and fleeting, but it does not lead to fulfillment, satisfaction, and *joy*, which is permanent and long lived.

- **Believing that you have worked too hard to get here.** There are only two ways to get to *thriving*: (1) you are fortunate enough to be born into financial and positional wealth, or (2) you work hard to get there. The reality is this: once you move up and experience higher levels, you do not normally want to move back down. Why? Because each level brings a new set of experiences, freedoms, and excitement. Moving to *thriving* on one's own is an accomplishment in and of itself. The thought of potentially giving something up to move to something more can seem incomprehensible or a pipe dream. Although it may seem impossible to grasp the reality of something more than *thriving*, this other reality is not a pipe dream, a lie, or a false hope—it is real. Hopefully, as we talked about *flourishing*, you noticed this and are starting to agree.

ACCELERATORS AND BARRIERS TO FLOURISHING

ACCELERATORS in the FLOURISHING level

What can help keep you focused on *Flourishing*?

- **Experiencing** flourishing. Eric Liddell (yes, him again—I told you he is one of my only human heroes) made a profound statement that captured my imagination when I saw the movie for the first time when I was in my twenties. I recall he said, "In the dust of defeat as well as the laurels of victory there is a glory to be found if one has done his best. God made me fast. And when I run, I feel His pleasure."[20]

---

20 *Chariots of Fire* (Enigma Productions, 1981).

> How about you? When have you done something that's at the intersection of your gifting, your experience, your contribution, and your passion where you know you contributed value to those around you? I asked this prior, and I will ask again: when have you felt God's pleasure? Stated differently: when you have felt joy and felt completely and utterly fulfilled and satisfied?

This is what it means to experience *flourishing*. It is difficult to describe in concrete terms what it means, but when you experience *flourishing* in your life, you just know it. I asked a mentor friend of mine who was known for recruiting young people with limited life experience and helping them grow, learn, and develop into successful, seasoned leaders what he looked for in these young people. After sharing with me for ten to fifteen minutes, he removed his glasses, sat back in his chair, sighed, and said, "The reality is, I just know it when I see it." It is the same when you experience *flourishing*.

- **You do it regardless of compensation.** Chances are, you are already doing something you are *flourishing* in for FREE. A few years ago, when I was struggling—I mean really struggling—with what to do with my career, my wife, Tiffani, asked me one of those questions that makes you feel like you just got punched in the gut by the heavy-weight boxing champion of the world, but while wearing the softest pillows possible on his hands. Her question took my breath away, but it did not have the bruising and pain that would have otherwise lasted for days. I had been working at and associated with the same organization for many years. I felt that God had released me from any kind of further obligation that I may have owed to this organization out of loyalty and dedication. My friends, my wife, my kids, and my work colleagues all knew that it was time for me to move on, but I was afraid. Yes, I was afraid because I did not have the confidence to do what I really wanted to do. Tiffani asked me the knock-out blow question, "What do you love doing that you don't get compensated for, that contributes to others' lives, and that you could see yourself doing for the rest of your career?" Both of us knew the answer. For years, whenever I was given the opportunity to write, speak, collaborate with leaders, facilitate leadership teams, and coach leaders, I knew that was when I was *flourishing*. How do I know that I loved doing this? Because I did these things whenever I was given the opportunity—I poured my head, heart, and energy into it, and I did it regardless of compensation or not.

- **Fear motivates, not immobilizes, you.** One of my favorite quotes of all time is the quote on courage by Franklin D. Roosevelt when he said, "Courage is not the absence of fear, but rather the assessment that something else is more important than fear."[21] I have read these words and derivatives of these words from President Roosevelt's quote many times over the years. I have also heard these words spoken at graduations, during television shows, in movies, in books, and on and on. It is so easy to say these words, especially when things are going well or fear is not debilitating you or keeping you from acting. As I was writing this section, I became curious as to the historical context under which President Roosevelt spoke these now famous words.

---

21   Source widely attributed to Franklin D. Roosevelt.

The United States had just come through World War 1 and was in the throes of the Great Depression. Unemployment was rampant. Food was scarce. The stock market had crashed. Money and savings were depleted or close to depleted. Hope was all but lost. The country was facing unprecedented difficulty, and the country was looking for something to believe in. This was the historical backdrop by which President Roosevelt spoke these words.

In our Western society, what are we taught from the time we are children? We are taught not to be afraid. "The only thing to fear is fear itself."[22] Face our fears, overcome our fears...but we all experience fear. I am convinced that fear is a universal emotion, along with happiness, sadness, and a handful of others. If fear is a universal emotion, then what should be our response to it? God gave us fear to help alert us and to help us escape those situations that are truly life threatening. If I am walking in the woods and a large brown grizzly bear comes across my path, then proceeds to stand up, wave his paws, and growl at me, I am certainly not going to choose that moment to exercise my courage in the face of fear. I am going to figure out the best and fastest way to get out of that situation. That is real fear, the fear for our lives when our lives really are in danger. I mentioned earlier that running into "paper walls" and "boxing shadows" triggers the same kind of fight-or-flight response that is triggered when we face real, physical danger, but we are not actually facing real, physical danger in those moments.

Fear is such a powerful emotion and one that can render a person immobile, but it can also motivate to action. Whatever your

---

22   Franklin D. Roosevelt, Inaugural Address (1933), https://www.whitehouse.gov/about-the-white-house/presidents/franklin-d-roosevelt/.

dream is, do not keep putting it off and wishing your life away, anticipating that it will happen "someday." Take one step today toward your dream. For additional resources on striving toward and reaching your dreams, I would highly recommend the book by Matthew Kelly titled *The Dream Manager*.[23]

BARRIERS in the FLOURISHING level

What can keep you from experiencing the *flourishing* life?

- **Believing that more is better.** In a world driven by money, wealth, and material possessions, it is so easy to fall into the mindset that more is better and accumulation leads to meaning, satisfaction, and happiness. Because the societal scorecard, even though it is not a physical scorecard, centers on making the *Forbes* "Wealthiest People in the World" or whatever the list is called this year, it is so easy to measure our personal worth and value in dollars and cents (or whatever your country's currency is). When it seems as though all the advertisements on television, in print, and online represent the rich and famous living the good life in their new cars, designer clothes, yachts whose sizes are compared to landmark buildings, and physically attractive men and women who seem to always be smiling and laughing, it is difficult not to make some comparison of our lives to theirs. These advertising companies are paid copious amounts of money to get the public to believe the life they are representing is the only life that is worth pursuing.

---

23   Matthew Kelly, *The Dream Manager* (New York: Beacon Publishing/ Hyperion, 2007).

I have been to many countries in Africa over two dozen times. I have seen the extremes of poverty and wealth in these countries. One of the interesting things I have learned in my time in Africa is that the same advertising and representation of a life that we do not currently have exists there as it does in any Western country. The same advertising strategies are employed in the poorest areas of the world as they are in the richest areas. Why? Because the world itself, regardless of what part of the world, struggles to define what is important and what brings true satisfaction and self-worth.

Each of us—you and me—is created with a hole in our soul, a hole that can only be filled with ONE thing. And that ONE thing is found with a relationship with our Creator. Without that relationship, we will try everything and anything possible to fill that hole in our lives—money, possessions, power, position, career, alcohol, drugs, thrill-seeking activities, volunteer work, meditation, religion, hobbies, sex, and the list goes on and on. Does filling this hole with a relationship with our Creator automatically "cure" the desire for these other things? Yes and no. Yes, because the hole is filled with that which it was intended to be filled. And no, because it is very possible that we may have created habits, hunger, or a life path that may have to be addressed and changed once our soul is satisfied. The bottom line for the barrier of "believing that *more* is better" is this: *more* is not always better. Sometimes *more* is just *more*. Sometimes *more* is *less*. And much of the time, *less* is *more*.

- **Fear of the unknown.** Fear is such a powerful motivator, and it can also be a barrier in our lives. Fear can move us to action and to accomplish feats that have no logical explanation. And fear can render us immobilized, paralyzed, and sitting in a corner sucking our fingers, wishing that the big bad monsters would just go away. One of the common characteristics of a *thriving* person is success—monetary, career, possessions, and so forth. Moving to *flourishing* often means intentionally deciding to change the path we are on in life. The *thriving* path leads to greater success as defined by having *more* and *better* things. The *flourishing* path will lead to greater meaning, fulfillment, and satisfaction but may lead to *less* things. Although the concept of experiencing the *flourishing* life may sound attractive and that it would be an amazing experience, the reality is that the fear of not knowing what you may have to give up because of moving from the *thriving* level to the *flourishing* level may be too great to overcome. It is possible to make the move, but you must be aware of and know that it often requires an intentional choice, or a series of choices, to change paths.

- **Lack of support and encouragement.** When you make the decision to move from the *thriving* level to the journey of *flourishing*, the reception and reaction to those in your life near and dear to you may surprise you. Please be aware of this as you make the decision to pursue this journey. Those in your life who were your greatest support and cheerleaders in your *thriving* journey may become your greatest critics and naysayers as you pursue your *flourishing* journey. Be prepared for anything. Why? It ties into the other barriers to *flourishing*—those around you have their own fears, their own opinions, and their own definitions of how life should be lived. The *flourishing* journey is not the norm—it is making the choice to push off the conventional and pursue your dreams, your hopes, your desires, and what is most important to you in life. This will surprise people—not *may* surprise people; it *will* surprise people. Many people will not know what to do with your decisions and choices. Some will be extremely supportive at first; however, if your life does not return to some kind of "normalcy" as they define it, those same voices could turn critical and increasingly vocal about their opinions of what they think you should do next. It is important to make sure that you ground yourself and are fully committed to this journey before you make the decision. If you are married and have a family, you need the commitment and the support of your spouse before you throw off the conventional, the consistent, and the predictable for a life that could be anything but those things. There will be days when you want to give up, like you made a mistake, like this just isn't worth the risk and the cost, but please keep pressing on as long as this is the life's journey you want to pursue and have made the intentional choice to pursue.

CHAPTER 7

Extraordinary Choices

*I*F YOU WANT *to live an extraordinary life, you must make extraordinary choices.* These choices are often unconventional, unexpected, and not the norm. Let me provide you with an actual example of what I mean by this.

I was coaching a young leader with amazing potential just recently. We were discussing his financial goals and dreams for his life. This young leader had laid out in detail how much he wanted to be earning and what positions he wanted to attain by certain ages in his life. He also discussed how much he wanted to have saved, his dream home, his dream cars, and his dream vacations. From knowing this leader well, I also know that having flexibility and freedom is a high value for him. So I asked him how his desire for flexibility and freedom played into his dreams. He made a comment that I have heard from many other leaders over the years: he said he would get to experience that in retirement. I asked him if he wanted to wait that long to experience that. He said that he did not, but that was just the way life was. After some discussion back and forth, I finally asked him if I could challenge him to consider one thing as regards his financial planning: if you want to live like

93

no one else is living, then you must live like no one else is living; if you want to do what no one else is doing, then you must do what no one else is doing. I challenged him to live his younger years with more discipline and sacrifice so he could live sooner than later with more flexibility and freedom than others may have.

The journey to a *flourishing* life is all about this conversation I had with this young leader. The choice to live a *flourishing* life is making the choice to live like no one else is living. Living a *flourishing* life is making the intentional choice to live your story differently and to make intentional choices that lead to a life that is different from what you have been living. Living a *flourishing* life is a life of intentionality where purpose, meaning, contributing to others, pursuing your calling, and surrendering to what God has prepared and equipped you to do become your life's focus and journey.

Before we move into the next part of our journey together, let's pause for a moment and look at our map so we know where we have been and where we are going next. We are concluding Part I, where we looked at the Flourishing Life Model. Part III of this book focuses on making the choices and integrating the lessons into your life that we just examined in Part I. Part II, the next part of this book, is my sharing part of my story with you to provide you with the hope that no matter what you have experienced, what you have done, how old you are, or where you are in your own life's journey, there is always a way to write a different ending to your story. My hope, as you read, is that you see your own story in mine and come to realize that there is always a path to intentionally choose a *flourishing* life for you and your journey.

PART II

THE STORY

CHAPTER 8

The Story

WE HAVE ONLY one life to live. There is only one *you* in life, which is why it is so critical and so important to live your best life possible.

Life is both the giver of great surprises and the giver of great disappointments. Life gives, but it also takes away. Life contributes, but it also consumes. My life is no exception to this, as I am sure your life is not an exception to this either. As I share my story with you, I encourage you to do the following two things as you think about your own story. First, if there are parts of your story that were painful or especially challenging, pause and ask yourself if you need to talk with someone about your experience. You may uncover areas of your story where you may need to work on forgiveness, you may need to forgive yourself, or you may need to ask someone to help you work through some healing for yourself. Second, as you think about your story, ask yourself where you are on the model in your own life. Where are you *diminished*, have given up, and need to hope again? Where are you *surviving*, realize that something is just not working for you anymore, and need the courage to try again? Where are you *striving* and need the encouragement and the support to keep going and keep pressing on? Where are you *thriving*, but the sense of fulfillment and satisfaction either is waning or just isn't there any longer, and you know it is time to stop climbing the ladder? Where are you *flourishing*, and what other areas of your life do you desire to *flourish* but are not yet?

As you read my story, here is what you will find: not every role in my life is *flourishing*. What? you may say. It isn't? No, it isn't. I promised you real, authentic, and practical. Not every role in my life is *flourishing*; however, my mindset and my commitment are to pursue a *flourishing* life *by role* and *as a whole* in my life for the rest of my life because I am convinced there is no better way to live for me...and for *you*! I may never reach my desire of having every role *flourishing*; however, I have spent so much of my life pursuing a *thriving* life, and I realize now how empty, unfulfilled, and unsatisfied that left me. I am committed to pursuing a *flourishing* life for the rest of my journey, as long as God gives me on this earth. My hope above all else as you read my story is that you examine your own story, and you are encouraged, energized, and filled with hope to pursue *flourishing* in your own story!

My life began as every life—with birth. I was born into a typical middle-class family in the Midwest. My dad was a youth pastor and was studying in seminary when I was born. My mom was an elementary school teacher. We lived in a small house in one of the suburbs of Chicago. I was born in a small town in Indiana while my parents were visiting my grandparents over Christmas. Yes, I was born the day after Christmas, and my mom went into labor on Christmas Eve, something I heard about every Christmas thereafter until she passed away. We lived near Chicago and in southern Wisconsin until I was four years old, when we relocated to a small lake community in northern Indiana, where I lived until I was twenty-one years old. Small-town life defined my existence during my childhood. We moved to Indiana because my dad bought into a business in a town about thirty minutes from where we lived.

I will never forget what happened in August of the summer when I was fourteen years old. During a getaway with my dad, we were swimming in the pool at the hotel and having a good time splashing around, and I was practicing cannonballs, which the other people using the pool were so (non)appreciative of me doing. For years, I thought they were rating my cannonballs when they would hold a finger on each hand. On a scale of 1 to 10, I thought I was amazing when I thought they were giving me an eleven! Only when I got a little older did I think back on that and realize that to get an eleven, they would probably have held up two different fingers than the ones they would hold up to me. Oh well, I had fun even though they did not, apparently, enjoy being splashed every time I jumped into the pool.

As my dad and I were wrestling around, he noticed that tiny red "dots" had appeared all over my arms, chest, stomach, and back. I got out of the pool and noticed that my legs were covered as well. We dried off and went back to our room, where I felt a bump on the inside of my cheek with my tongue. When I opened my mouth to have a peek, I didn't just see one blood blister; I saw over twenty.

When we arrived home, my mom took one look at me (this was before the days of cell phones, so the first she knew of this was when I arrived back home) and called our family doctor, Dr. Hughes. He told us he did not have a diagnosis but that something was wrong and to drive to a regional hospital, where he arranged for me to be under the care of a pediatric hematologist/oncologist. Just the word "oncologist" sent a wave of shock and fear through my parents (I do not remember hearing that word, or if I did, I did not know what it meant, so I was oblivious to the seriousness of what was about to happen to me). After we arrived, they drew blood and started running tests.

First thing the next morning—my first full day in the hospital— the pediatric hematologist/oncologist came into my room. He had the typical white lab coat attire, but he was different than any doctor I had ever met. He started out by coming over to me, extending his hand to shake mine, putting his other arm on my shoulder, and saying, "Hi, my name is Jim. You must be Matt. I am so glad to meet you!" I will never forget Dr. Hill. He immediately put me at ease with his approach and demeanor. He was warm, friendly, and down to earth.

Jim sat on the side of my bed as I lay on it, and he talked with me for a few minutes. He wanted to hear the story of how I ended up at the hospital. After a while, he told me that he and the nurses were going to take good care of me and do their best to figure out what was going on, get me better, and get me back in the weight room and on the soccer field again. Jim privately shared with my parents that the blood work results had come back, and initial indications were pointing to a diagnosis of leukemia. My parents later told me it was like the heavy-weight boxing champion of the world had just punched them a thousand times in the gut. They both felt like yelling, crying, and throwing up. Jim did say that the diagnosis could only be confirmed or disproven by doing a bone marrow test, which meant he had to get a sample of my bone marrow from either my hip or my chest. They all thought it would be easier and less cosmetically intrusive to go in through my hip instead of my chest.

After the agonizing bone marrow test was finished, Jim told my parents that he hoped to have the results back that same day or by the next morning at the latest. The day seemed to drag on forever, and we did not see Jim. We were getting ready to turn in for the night when around 9:30 p.m., Jim stuck his head in the door. He came in my room, and he shared with all of us—yes, I got to be part of the conversation this time—that the bone marrow test results had come back and the result of the test was negative. I did *not* have leukemia. He said that he spent most of the day doing research and contacting other, larger hospitals and research hospitals trying to figure out what could be going on if it wasn't leukemia. He said that he was certain that I had a rare blood disease called idiopathic thrombocytopenia purpura, or ITP for short. In 1988, ITP was still a rare diagnosis (it is much more common today).

The short and straightforward way to describe ITP is this: my body turned on itself and saw its own platelets as objects to be destroyed. This was an issue if I ever wanted to or needed to stop bleeding if I was ever cut or injured. I needed my platelets! Jim said that when he saw my blood work results, he said that he had never seen or heard of anyone being admitted with a platelet count as low as mine.

The good news, Jim said, was that ITP could be treated in such a way as to protect my body's platelets from being destroyed. The bad news was that the treatment, which was a blood by-product called gamma globulin administered through an IV line, was not a cure, and there was no knowing if the treatment results would last a day, a month, a year, or forever. Nonetheless, we had hope, and my journey of *surviving* was just beginning and would last for the next twelve months.

The next morning, the nurses came in, put in an IV line, and prepared me for the treatment. They told me it would take about six to eight hours for the treatment to be completely injected into me. The day of the treatment was fine. I even got milkshakes and played cards with the nurses (I may or may not have won $10 at poker). The aftereffects that night were awful, with vomiting and an agonizing headache. Early the next morning, the mobile blood cart came into my room to draw blood. This day we would know whether the treatment the day prior was effective or not. A couple of hours later, Jim came into my room to check on me and see how I was doing. He shared with my parents and me that my platelet count had risen above the critical threshold. I was originally admitted to the hospital with a platelet count of less than 1,000 (for reference, a healthy individual has a platelet count of 150,000–400,000). The day after my treatment, my count had risen to 25,000—not enough to go home but enough that I was out of danger of spontaneously bleeding to death.

Jim said that the plan was to test my blood daily and see which way my count went from that day. The good news was that the treatment was working! The sad news was that, on average, for the first six months or so, the treatments provided me with three to five days of an elevated count before it would quite quickly fall back into the critical zone of less than 25,000. Six months into the treatments, we figured out that if I drank about two gallons of water during my six- to eight-hour treatment, I would not get a headache or vomit. This was amazing news. The unwelcome news was that I had to get up and pee every fifteen minutes all day.

I spent the first five weeks in the hospital. After that, my routine for the better part of the next year was the following: be admitted to the hospital, get treatment during the day, stay overnight, get a terrible headache and vomit all night (for the first six months), go home for a few days while being completely restricted from activities, get my blood tested every other day, and when my platelet count dropped under 25,000, do it all over again. I was in the hospital weekly for the first six months. During the second six months, the treatments started lasting longer, and I was able to go two, sometimes three, weeks at a time in between treatments.

After the initial shock wore off and a routine of treatment, ill-reaction, testing, drop in count, back to the hospital, treatment—wash, rinse, dry, repeat—became my new reality, so did something else: *anger.* I became angry. It was bad enough that I was missing soccer season, but missing soccer season ran into missing the start of school. I was going into my freshman year of high school, and I was missing it. And this year was going to be different than any other school year yet, doggone it. I was disciplined, I had worked my tail off, and I had gotten out of bed early in the morning every day to work out. Up until this school year, I was the overweight, uncoordinated kid chosen last in gym class. That was my reality, but that was all about to change because I had worked my butt off over the past year. Now I was helplessly watching it all fade away. Using the terminology of the model, I had decided to start *striving* to get into better shape and improve enough to experience *thriving* in high school sports, especially soccer and basketball.

At first, I was disappointed, then sad, and then angry, with a little bitterness mixed in for good measure. I was angry that my activities were restricted, and I was angry that I was missing school. I was restricted to a bed because of the risk of falling or hitting my head when my platelet count was so low, along with the accompanying risk of not being able to stop bleeding. I was angry at my parents for listening to the doctors. I was angry at God for bringing this upon me. For months, I carried this anger.

How about you? Do you resonate with these emotions? Think of a time when you had tried hard, you had prepared yourself, you had worked your butt off and then something happened, and everything fell apart in front of your eyes. Not only did you not get what you had hoped for, but you also experienced a setback, a failure, or a major disappointment.

These kinds of setbacks can send you into a tailspin where you may lose hope, or you may decide that it is just not worth trying any longer. So you give up. You quit. You walk away from what you were doing, or you walk away from a relationship, or you walk away from God. You decide that *striving* is not worth it any longer, and you were better off *surviving*, or even worse, *diminished.* I understand. I knew what that was like when I was a teenager, and I have experienced it many times since. Please do not give up! Keep moving. Keep pressing on. Make the intentional choice to keep on your journey.

CHAPTER 9

The Turning Point

Six months into my treatments, in the middle of a wintry night at 2:00 a.m. in a hospital room all by myself, I was crawling back into bed after vomiting for the fifth or sixth time. I only remember the time because there was a clock in my room hanging over my television, which was always in plain sight. As I was crawling back into bed, this profound thought hit me like I had just run into a brick wall. The thought went something like this: "Here I am angry with God—the One who could heal me if He chose to heal me. This does not make any sense." Then I prayed, "God, I have been angry and have been blaming You for this illness. I am so sorry. I am finished being angry and blaming You. I give my life to You. Please do with me as You will and use me as You see fit." That was it. Quite simple and short. And then I drifted off to sleep.

Over the years, people have asked if I was healed that night. It is one of those questions that quite honestly is not a simple yes or no answer—it is more complex, and it is deeper than a simple yes or no, at least it is for me. I understand that when I am asked this question, most people are not necessarily wanting to hear the whole story or the deeper meaning that I have associated with it.

I have learned over time to give a response that is something like this: "I was not healed physically, but my heart was healed." I did not have this terminology then, but I realize now that what happened was this. That night, I made the intentional decision, by surrendering my life to God, to pursue a *flourishing* life no matter what was happening to me. Did I do that perfectly from that night on? Not at all. However, I never forgot that prayer and what happened to me that night. I was in a mental rut up to that point that kept me in *surviving* mode—even *diminished* mode because I had given up on many things that were important to me. From that night until the illness mysteriously went away about six months after that night, my perspective completely changed. I stopped focusing on me—what I was missing, what I had lost, what I was suffering, or how unfair this was to me. My perspective shifted from "This is all about me" to "What can I learn and how can I serve and help others?"

How about you? Can you relate? When was the last time you were going through a challenging time and life was throwing her fury at you? What were you focused on during that? Were you focused on how "unfair" or how "unjust" life was?

It is in the valleys of life when we are facing challenges, failures, setbacks, and pain that reveal where we are on our journey. If we choose to focus on ourselves and how "unfair" life is being, we are in the *surviving* level, or even worse, if we have given up because we may be at the *diminished* level. When we make the intentional choice to stop focusing on how "unfair" life is and stop having a "victim's mindset," then we can adopt a *flourishing* mindset by choosing to focus outward, focus on others, give back, choose hope, and choose to keep moving and living again.

A little more than twelve months after everything started, I had a treatment, like normal. The next day, I had a blood test, and my platelet count had risen substantially—more than usual. Over the next week, I got my routine tests every other or second day. To my parents', my doctors', and my surprise, my platelet count did not drop. At first, it dropped a little, then it held steady, and then it began to rise—yes, RISE! We gradually stretched the testing to weekly, then every other week, and then monthly. About a year after I met Jim, the blood disease left. Jim promised me that he would do everything he could do to figure out what was making me ill and then figure out how to treat me and get me back to living a normal life again. Jim did exactly what he said he would do the first time he met me. Although he knew how to treat it, he did not inherently have the capability, expertise, or ability to heal me. That could only come from God. Over time, we eventually got to annual blood testing, and that has been the case for me ever since. To this day, my platelet count usually registers between 120,000 and 150,000, but it also occasionally drops below 100,000. A minor cut for me still turns into a bloody mess, and what would result in a slight bruise for the average person looks like I was in a bar fight, which is great for storytelling but not so great for competing in a beauty contest!

As I reflect on this part of my story now, God used this experience to slow me down and to get my attention. It was during this year that I made the decision to give my life to Jesus and follow Him. Even though I surrendered my life to Him, I did not know—in my teenage immaturity and lack of understanding—exactly what that meant. I only knew that I changed my mindset and communicated that I was open to whatever God had for me in my life. It was a miracle that I survived this illness. I would not begin to understand what God had for me until after the illness had passed, and I will tell you more about that in the next chapter.

> **How about you? What is something that happened in your life that you could not make sense of or explain? It does not have to be something as dramatic as an illness, but it may have been. It may have been something more subtle or even something that was exciting and joyous for you! Did you ever stop to think that God was trying to get your attention?**

I am not one of those people who think that every challenging or every exciting situation we face in life is a way for God to get our attention because sometimes it is just the result of good (or poor) decision making on our part. However, I do believe that when we experience something out of the normal, we should pay attention and see, just see, if there is a bigger reason or purpose for what we are experiencing.

> **How about you? Have there been times in your life where a greater purpose or message was intended for you? What were those messages? It is these messages that are so easy to miss because life keeps moving so quickly. Think about your own story and document those messages so you have them to reflect on and learn from as your story continues to develop.**

We will revisit this in Part III where we talk about application and integration.

CHAPTER 10

The Birth of a Dream

ROUGHLY A MONTH after my restrictions were lifted, it was time for my church's annual youth camp. I was so excited that I was allowed to go, be with my friends, and participate in the week's activities.

The theme of that week was about evaluating the condition of our heart—as in our attitude, our mindset, our beliefs, and our convictions. I honestly do not know if I would have understood the message or even cared; however, do you remember what happened to me about six months prior in the middle of the night in my hospital room? Because of that night six months prior at 2:00 a.m. in the hospital bed, I knew exactly what this speaker was saying. I am not an emotionally expressive person, but suddenly, I became overwhelmed with emotion. I had big tears come to my eyes. I knew that in those moments, it was not really the speaker speaking to me anymore—it was God speaking to my heart. In the moments that followed, I repeated the same prayer to God that I prayed six months prior that I wanted Him to use me however He saw fit.

It was at this camp that I believe God put the birth of a dream in my heart and mind. The dream was that someday, I would be doing what this speaker did. That night, I did not have any details, a map or game plan was not given to me, and I had no idea what step, if any, I was supposed to take. Without knowing exactly what I was supposed to do, I took one step—I committed my life to God and surrendered to whatever He had for me, not knowing specifically what it was that I was committing to at the time. As time went on, I took more steps by engaging in writing, teaching, and facilitating groups. I have spent the last thirty-two years taking steps by learning, studying, growing, and practicing as much as I could to grow in these skills and competencies.

> How about you? When were you asked to "take a step" without fully knowing what you were being asked to do? Perhaps you are being asked to take a step—a step of faith—right now? Whatever it is in any area of your life where you feel you are being asked to take a step—just one step—what is it? What is keeping you from taking that step?

Be honest with yourself—your fears, your hesitancy—and then do it! Take that first step, whatever it may be. For you, your first step may be making that decision that you have been putting off for far too long. Or maybe your first step is to make that phone call or have that difficult conversation that you know you need to have. Or perhaps your first step is to enroll in that class or take that training that you have been wanting to take for quite some time. Or maybe your first step is making the choice to get help or get coaching for an area of your life that you have been struggling with. Or perhaps your first step is a much bigger step, like deciding to leave a role where you know you are barely *surviving*, and you know it is time to move on to something else. The next part of the story will continue the journey of taking steps in the pursuit of a *flourishing* life.

CHAPTER 11

Who Am I? Depression and Identity

AFTER MY ILLNESS, I struggled with who I was and where I fit in. I did not think the same or have the same perspective on life that I had prior to my illness. Everything was different for me. I have often said that my childhood ended during the year that I had my blood disease. I was a teenager who felt like a misfit. I did not know where I fit. I did not yet know who I was or what my identity was as a person.

When I finished high school and attended college, my goal was not to get an education or have a great college experience. No, it was to beat my mom's college GPA. Yes, that was my motivation to get good grades. This meant I would have to get a GPA of 4.0 because she got a 3.98. Do you know what I learned from obsessing over my grades for four years in college to reach that goal? I realized, years later, that the cost and sacrifice of spending four years in college barely making any friends, not experiencing student life (I think I may have gone to one, maybe two, sports games while I was in college), and putting everything and everyone else in a lower priority position than my grades, was a huge cost. A cost that turned into regret once I became aware of how great the cost was in my life.

Why do I share this with you? My life up until the moment when I was taking the reins of our family business consisted of school. That was it. I knew how to succeed in school, and I was an exceptionally good student. Experiencing academic success gave me two things: (1) false confidence and (2) intellectual arrogance. Since I had academic success, I falsely believed that I could accomplish anything I wanted to accomplish on my own. I thought I was living a *flourishing* life, but I realize now that while I was *thriving* in school, I was barely *surviving* in other areas of my life because of the huge sacrifices I had made.

How about you? Have you ever experienced this? You worked so hard to accomplish something you thought would bring you fulfillment and satisfaction— *flourishing*. You accomplish what you sacrificed so much to achieve, and you feel fulfilled and satisfied, but it was short lived, and you wound up facing the reality that many other areas of your life were barely *surviving*.

After college, in a series of events that I never saw coming, I took over the reins of the family business. I thought I would experience smashingly good business success, especially since that is what I studied in college. For a minute, I experienced a *thriving* life, but then I realized how wrong I was once again. And I do not mean a little wrong; I mean very, *very* wrong. Within three months of taking over, I discovered problem after problem after problem that was not previously known to me and rendered the business insolvent. Tiffani and I had been married for less than a year, and I faced the first major failure of my life and it was a big one: *the family business had failed.*

I went from *thriving* to barely *surviving* in three short months. The first thing to go was sleep—sleepless nights became the norm for me. Then anxiety, followed quickly by panic attacks. I did not know any of this terminology at the time I was experiencing it. If you have never experienced a panic attack, the best way to describe it is like this: imagine someone tells you to lie down on the floor on your back, then they drop a fifty-pound bag of dry concrete on your gut, and they say, "Now take a deep breath." That does not work! Every time the phone would ring at my office, I would run to the toilet and vomit. Lucky for me, I had a toilet right next to my office. After two months of this, I stopped getting out of bed, or if I did, I would not go to the office. Somehow, I made it through my first wedding anniversary, Thanksgiving, and Christmas. But three weeks into the new year, I could not face life any longer. The journey from *thriving* to *surviving* was sliding very quickly to *diminishing.* I felt helpless. I felt hopeless.

How about you? Have you ever experienced a time when you felt helpless or, worse yet, hopeless? I understand what that feels like.

Just a short eight months after taking over the family business, I woke up after sleeping the entire night. I had my first good night's sleep in months because I had decided that would be my final day on earth. I had decided to end my life. My journey had arrived at the *diminishing* level. I got out of bed, showered, dressed, and went to my office—for the first time in months. I sat down at my desk and pulled out three pieces of paper to write three letters—to my bride, my mom (whom I had hired to come work for me), and my little brother (whom I felt responsible for like a father for his son). I never penned one word. Not one. As I was preparing to write, the thought crossed my mind that my parents had taken out a life insurance policy on me when I was young, but I did not know any of the details about it. Rather than calling the agent (a life-long friend of my mom's), I decided to drive the three blocks to his office to talk to him in person about the policy. He happened to be in and he happened to be available. We talked for about fifteen to twenty minutes, and then I left to go back to my office.

As I walked in the door of my office, my mom greeted me and said, "Let's go out for tea," which was not unusual—we would often go for tea to get away from the constant barrage of running a business. This time, however, she added, "I will drive." Now, this was odd—I always drove. I was in no shape to argue, so she drove. A mile into our drive on our way to our local tea hangout, Mom got into the turn lane at the only major thoroughfare in town. I asked her where we were going. She said, "To see a friend." I did not know it then, but as soon as I left my life insurance agent's office, he picked up the phone and called my mom. I do not know the exact conversation, but I have been able to piece together enough of it through the years to know it went something like this: "Jean [my mom's name], I know things are a mess, and you are trying to figure out what to do, but none of that matters right now. I just spent time with your son, and if you do not do something today, he will not be here tomorrow." She hung up the phone and then proceeded to call the only other person she knew who had been through something similar ten years prior. He was a friend of my mom from high school who was now a successful businessperson in town. He just happened to be in his office and had time to give us. He told her to bring me right over.

As she moved into the lane to turn into his office, I asked her why she was turning into his office. She responded simply to me,

"Because you need help, and he understands what you are going through." We spent six hours with him that day, unpacking everything that had happened over the prior years. At the end of our time, he did not promise to fix everything or to take away the pain. He simply said, "I will walk with you through this." And he did. I was immediately put into psychiatric care and diagnosed with clinical depression with suicidal risk. My mom's and my new friend called my wife, met with her, and told her everything that was happening. My journey up from *diminishing* was about to begin.

CHAPTER 12

The Journey from *Diminishing*

I HAVE BEEN ASKED over the years why this successful business-person called Tiffani and talked with her—how did she not know what was going on? The simple and shameful answer is this: I had no clue how to be a husband. I thought it was my "duty" to be macho and act like everything was fine. My wife knew there were issues, but she had no idea how bad they truly were. I thought it was somehow my duty to act like nothing was wrong or to minimize the trouble we were experiencing. I thought it was my duty to protect my wife from all the harmful stuff. I thought that being a man meant that you could not reveal your weaknesses or your vulnerabilities. I thought to be a good husband meant that you had to portray a certain image to your wife that reflected strength, confidence, and machismo. I thought that to be a good husband, I had to portray a *thriving* life to my wife, regardless of how I was feeling and regardless of what reality really was. I had no clue.

Rather than protecting Tiffani through all of this, years later, she shared with me that she felt shut out of my life. She felt like she could observe everything that was going on but as though watching through a glass house where she could see people talking, and she knew there were problems, but she could not hear anything that was said. In my ignorance, my arrogance, and my naiveness, I wound up doing exactly the opposite of what I intended to do: I took away the opportunity for her to be engaged with me, I took away the opportunity for us to bond as spouses, and I hurt her badly. I took away the opportunity for Tiffani to be on the journey with me from *thriving* down to *surviving*, and finally, down to *diminishing*. I have thought many times since this what would have happened had I chosen to be real with my wife and have her fully engaged with me on the journey. Would I have descended so low? Would I have wound up at the *diminishing* level? Would I have gotten to the point where I was seriously considering ending my life? I will never know the answer to this, *but I wonder.*

Note to all husbands reading this: It is never a clever idea to pretend or hide from your wife. They know! Be transparent and walk through life together, experiencing the good and the bad, the beautiful and the ugly. If you are identifying areas of your life where you are moving down from *thriving* to *surviving* or even to *diminishing*, please engage your spouse in your journey...and do it now! Do what I was not capable of doing and ask your spouse and others for help so you do not continue to spiral downward in your own journey.

Note to everyone reading this: This plea does not apply just to husbands reading this! Regardless of your marital status, gender, or any other demographic, make the intentional choice to allow others to join you on your life's journey because everyone faces times in life where you experience *thriving* or *flourishing*, and you need others to be with you to celebrate and help keep you balanced. And everyone experiences times in life where you feel like you are barely *surviving*, or you are experiencing times of *diminishing* and you feel like you are barely holding on. In these times, you need people in your life more than ever who care about and love you to walk with you and help you weather those storms.

Let's continue our journey through identity development, which is critical to allowing people into your life, especially when life's journey is difficult.

THE JOURNEY TO A NEW IDENTITY

While I was out of the business healing and getting help, I met with a counselor, John, multiple times per week. Tiffani and I wound up working with this counselor for six years as he helped us learn who we were both as individuals and as a couple. It was during these years in counseling that Tiffani and I had an opportunity for what I affectionately refer to as a "do-over" without having to go through the pain and tragedy of having an actual ending first. Tiffani and I both thought that after seven years of dating before we married, we really knew each other. Again, wow, were we wrong! We were both so naive and clueless as to the baggage, the assumptions, the narratives, and how our unique stories that we each brought into the marriage were already starting to erode the relationship, and that was only a year and a half into it.

> **How about you? Are you in a marriage or relationship that you thought would be something much more than it is? Do not give up! There is always hope. Please seek the help of a wise counselor or mentor or friend—or all three.**

One of the most puzzling questions that John asked me within the first few months of starting counseling was a simple question. It was a short question but one for which I had no answer. The question was simply, "Who are you?" I looked at John with a blank stare and said, "What?" He repeated, "Who are you?" I said, "What do you mean?" He said again, "Who are you?" I hung my head and finally said, "I have no idea. I know what some people want me to be. But I have no idea how to answer your question." I will never forget John's response. He got up out of his chair, came over to me, put his arm around my shoulders, and gently said, "That is okay. That is fully what I expected you to say! We will figure it out together. I promise! I will walk with you every step of the way." John and a handful of other men invested in and poured time and energy into me, and they began to teach, mentor, and coach me. They taught me not just how to be a husband but also what it meant to be a man. What John and these other mentors did with me was to help me realize who I was.

I have been asked over the years what I learned from going through my depression and then coming back from it. There would not be enough pages or time to explain all the lessons I learned. So let me summarize it by saying this to you: we *all* experience highs and lows in life. Life gives us amazing experiences that we would love to repeat over and over; however, life also gives us brutal challenges and pain that we never desire to repeat again. Regardless of what you are experiencing or where you are on your journey from *diminishing* to *flourishing*, the point is this: do not go on your journey alone. Life is so short and precious. We are not promised tomorrow, and we do not know when our tomorrows will end. As painful as the *diminishing* and *surviving* levels of our journey may be, we need others on the journey with us.

How about you? Are you on this journey alone? If so, invite someone to be on the journey with you. If you have been keeping others—especially your spouse if

you are married—at arm's length, invite them into your journey, into your story, and do it today!

Now I'll dive into this in more depth and provide you with examples and guidance on how to do this.

SELF-AWARENESS AND OTHERS-AWARENESS LEARNING

Why share the painful journey of my depression and near-suicide with you? Because without the pain, hardship, valleys, and failures I have experienced in life, I am not who I am today. Without experiencing the *diminishing* level, I would not be able to describe to you what that experience is like. The same holds true for the other levels as well. I had hit rock bottom. By the grace and mercy of God, my journey began to move toward *thriving* and, eventually, toward *flourishing.* I am not saying that successes and mountaintops in life are not also meaningful because they are. I believe that based on who I am and how I am wired, God has used the pain and hardships in my life to shape and mold me in ways that just would not have been possible during the successes and mountaintops of life. For me, the greatest amount of self-learning and self-revelation I have learned in life has not come from my successes or my mountaintop experiences; it has come from the failures, the low times, and the deep trenches.

How about you? When have you learned the most about yourself? What experiences in your life contributed to greater self-awareness? If you have experiences and life learnings that are coming to mind

now, write them down. In Part III, we will visit the subject of "Your Story" more thoroughly.

When I was younger, I used to fear the lows and the valleys. However, what was fear in my twenties is now hopeful optimism in my late forties. Why? Because of everything new that can be learned and gained that I do not yet know about who I am. I have spent the last twenty-five years in an enthusiastic pursuit of understanding who I am and who others are. As Tiffani and I neared the end of our counseling with John, I became excited (Tiffani may call it obsessed, but I prefer excited) about pursuing additional training in understanding how I am wired because I knew I needed to understand myself better so I could also better understand her and others. Over the next decade, I pursued training and certification in nearly twenty personality, behavioral, and leadership assessments. This allowed me to better understand why I was so misunderstood and why I seemed to have a growing accumulation of broken relationships and relational destruction behind me. The more I learned about how I and others were wired, our preferences, our motivations, our strengths, and our weaknesses, the more I began to understand my journey and the more I wanted to understand others' journeys.

> **How about you? Who are you? If you do not know where to begin to answer this question, start with what is obvious that you know about yourself and work your way to the less obvious. Ask your family, friends, and coworkers for feedback. One reason knowing your story is so important is because your story is a great way to identify who you are.**

The journey to *flourishing* starts with knowing who you are and where you are on your journey. Once you know that, you can then begin to understand who others are and where they are on their journey. This is important because you need others on your journey with you toward *flourishing* just as others need you on theirs! The journey is what we will focus on in the next chapter.

In learning more about who I am, I discovered my natural wiring is driven, task-oriented, and goal motivated. In my pursuit of goals in life, I would inadvertently hurt people, disregard them, and ruin relationships, and I could not for the life of me figure out what was going on. As I grew in self-awareness, I had this dawning reality: my heart's desire was to pursue a *flourishing* life and help others do the same. However, because of my driven nature and utter obliviousness to others' journeys in life, I was having the opposite results for both me and them. I had to change. I wanted to change. I started to change. I will unpack this more for you in the next chapter.

CHAPTER 13

The Path Emerges

WHEN LIFE DEALS us circumstances that cannot be changed, you adjust and you deal with what you have been given. Likewise, the path to *flourishing* is never a straight-line journey. Never. It is possible to experience *flourishing* in one or more areas of life and experience *surviving* in others. There have been times in our married life when Tiffani and I were not *flourishing* in our marriage, but we were not just *surviving* either. We have always been committed to each other, which meant that we would do whatever it took—*surviving*, if that is what it took—but always keep our desired state of *flourishing* at the top of mind in our relationship. Over the years since we went through my depression, years of counseling, the traumatic birth experience of our first-born, and the eighteen months of recovery that followed his birth, there have been numerous other times where we have experienced everything from *flourishing* to *surviving*. Through it all, Tiffani and I have been blessed with opportunities to speak, counsel, and build relationships with many couples who were either preparing to get married or who were already married. I am a big believer that God never wastes pain or suffering in our lives; He redeems that to be used in ways we often cannot imagine.

I mentioned earlier about my personality and my natural wiring to drive hard, relentlessly pursue goals, and demand increasingly more of myself and others around me. There are times when my personality benefits me, but there are also times when it, unfortunately, works against me.

> **How about you? Can you think of times when how you are wired provides benefit to you? Can you also think of times when your wiring, unfortunately, works against you? If anything comes to mind, write it down. We will use this in Part III.**

I have spent the last twenty years focused on learning about and growing in my weaknesses, vulnerabilities, and blind spots because I knew that if I did not, my wiring would eventually lead to huge pain and destruction (relationally speaking) in my life. Since I can remember, I have had an inner drive for *more* and *better*; however, that desire for *more* and *better* was never satisfied. Never. Why? Because when you are driven by *more* and *better*, there is always *more* and *better* of everything. It is a never-ending pursuit that ultimately leads to frustration, disillusionment, anger, bitterness, and a sense of being constantly *unsatisfied*.

If someone said, "You will never be able to do that," my response was, "Oh yeah? Watch me!" And then I would dig in and double my efforts to prove them wrong. My basic philosophy has been that if having two of something is good, then having twenty or twenty-two hundred had to be better, right? This is why I am no longer allowed to go to warehouse shopping clubs like Sam's Club or Costco by myself! I was never satisfied...with anything. I always wanted *more* and *better*: *better* job or title, *more* money, *better* house, *better* cars, *more* influence, and bigger (*better*) platform. It was exhausting, and it did not lead to what I desired: *satisfaction* and *fulfillment*. In fact, it led to the opposite: being *unsatisfied* and *never fulfilled*.

How about you? Can you relate to this? When has this happened in your life's journey? If something comes to mind, write it down so you have it available for use in Part III.

While I was out of the business after my depression, a group of wise people collaborated with my mom to help relaunch the family business. The new company grew and expanded quite rapidly over the next decade. Eventually, as many family businesses experience, growth became difficult to sustain, and with increased growth comes increased risk. The risk became greater than the reward, and we made the gut-wrenching decision to sell.

After selling the family business in 2007, I joined the world of private equity, as I mentioned earlier. That was a completely new and different world for me, and I loved the challenges and experiences it provided me. I was able to collaborate with amazing leaders all over the world, I got to travel both domestically and internationally, and I learned from some of the smartest people I have ever met; however, it was not enough for me. I was not satisfied. I was *thriving* during most of my time, but toward the end, it felt like I was just *surviving*. After twelve years, I left private equity after feeling that God had called me to another opportunity. I went into banking as an executive at a local bank, only to discover that banking was not for me, and I knew it in the first week I was there. I was *thriving* on the outside (most of the time), but I was barely *surviving* on the inside. I lasted about a year, and then I left without having another job.

I took seven months off and focused on my marriage (which was also barely *surviving* because of all the changes, challenges, and my internal turmoil of feeling like I was a failure in many roles in life), my kids, and my relationship with God. I hired a professional coach, Tiffani and I began seeing a counselor again, I dived into the Bible, and I read two to three books per week, searching for answers to why I was never *satisfied*. The professional world and my "all or nothing, go big and then go bigger, *more*, and *better*" approach to life had taken its toll on our marriage and our family. Our counselor, Verlin, helped Tiffani and me begin to heal and grow again.

After seven months off, I joined my friend as an executive in his family business to help him build his team and his business. But the seed had been planted deep within me; I just did not understand it. After six months of *thriving* in my role with my friend, my role changed, and I knew my new role would mean that I would have to experience *surviving* once again (it was a role I knew I was not suited for, at least not long term). At the same time, my oldest son was diagnosed with testicular cancer at the age of nineteen (it was caught very early, and after surgery, he is currently cancer-free, thank God!), and my two and a half hours of commuting every day where I was missing much of my kids' school and extracurricular activities again began to take a toll on my family and mental state. After one year of working with my friend, we parted ways.

I had a friend who encouraged me to go "all-in" pursuing my dream. He did not know that he was telling me to go pursue a *flourishing* life and stop settling for roles where I was *surviving* or roles where I was *thriving* on the outside but merely *surviving* on the inside. My new path had emerged. I did not know what the new path on my journey would look like, but it had emerged, and I was ready to begin.

How about you? Have you experienced a time when a new path emerged on your journey and you knew it was time for a change? If something comes to mind, write it down. These journey changes are important parts of your story that we will explore in Part III.

Let's explore this dynamic even more and provide guidance for your own journey.

THE DREAM BECOMES A REALITY

My friend's encouragement to go "all-in" in pursuing my dream became the motivation to "burn the ships" (from the story I mentioned earlier about Cortés) and start my own company. I did just that. I started a business focused on leadership development, team building, coaching, and consulting. I also started writing the words that became what you now hold in your hands.

I had dreamed of writing and speaking for over thirty-two years. In those moments when I was considering what to do, I was not necessarily thinking through all the preparation I had experienced leading up to this day. Instead, the way I described it to my wife and to a handful of close friends was that I was excited, hopeful, and scared as hell. I have an incredibly supportive wife and kids, but I also have a desire to provide a life for them that is not a roller coaster of emotions and unknowns. I knew what "burning the ships" would mean: diving headfirst, all-in, up to my neck into the unknown, unpredictable, and the uncertain. I know how few new businesses survive, and I also know the statistics on how difficult it is to get a book published and, if it was published, how few books sell enough copies to put a dent into anyone's budgetary needs. I knew the statistics. I knew the odds. I knew how difficult this journey would be. But after months of prayer, talking with wise people who my wife and I trust and love, and after much thinking and analyzing (not to mention the sleepless nights, the headaches, the tears, the tension, the cold sweats, and the fear), my wife, kids, and I went all-in—together. For the first time in my professional life, we were doing this together. We were pursuing *flourishing* together.

For thirty-two years, I had a dream to write, speak, teach, and coach. I did not get serious about pursuing *flourishing* until I "burned my ships" and chose to pursue this new path all-in.

But now, as I stared my dream in the face, right between the eyes, I was scared—scared frozen to the point that I did not know if or how I would even take my first step. Even writing these words today scares the hell out of me! Because what if even though I took the leap of faith, I jumped in with both feet, and I "burned my ships" it does not work? What if I fail? What if my thirty-two-plus-year dream turns into a nightmare? Then I will have to pick myself up, adjust, pivot, and move on. Is that not what we do in life? But for now, I am pursuing a *flourishing* life full-on by pursuing what I had dreamed of pursuing for over thirty-two years, where God called me to this during a summer youth camp after spending a year with a rare blood illness.

How about you? Do you have a dream? Maybe it is a small dream, or maybe it is a big one. Regardless, do you have a dream? What is keeping you from pursuing it? Where are you barely *surviving* right now? Does your *surviving* have anything to do with that dream that you are not pursuing yet that could put you on a path to experiencing a *flourishing* life? Are you stuck in a role (or a series of roles) where you are capable and

successful (even hugely successful), but you know—
you just know—that you are "called" or "wired" to do
something else? If anything comes to mind, write it
down.

This is the difference between living at the *surviving* level versus
the *flourishing* level. Living at the *flourishing* level does not necessarily mean huge successes or making truckloads of money. Really?
Really. There are wonderfully successful people who have the title,
the position, and make lots of money who are miserable—who are
barely *surviving*.

How about you? Does this describe you? If so, what is
one step you can take right now to begin your journey
toward pursuing a *flourishing* life? Do you need to
have a "burn your ships" moment to get there? What is
keeping you from doing that?

In Part III, I am going to give practical steps you can take to
start your journey to a *flourishing* life.

PART III

INTEGRATION

CHAPTER 14

Integration Leads to Transformation

L ET'S REVIEW OUR journey. We started with the Flourishing Life Model where we explored the definitions of *diminishing*, *surviving*, *striving*, *thriving*, and *flourishing*. I encouraged you to evaluate your life by *role* and *as a whole* at each of these levels of the model. As I am sure you asked then and are asking now, "What do I do after I evaluate my life by *role* and *as a whole?*" Great question! That is the fundamental question I am going to answer for you in this concluding section, Part III, of the book.

After the model, I shared with you some of my story—my own journey from *diminishing* to *flourishing*. My aim in sharing my story was to provide you with a working example of what the journey looks like so you can identify your own story in my story. I also shared to give you hope—hope that no matter where you are on the model, or how old you are, or what your background, or what you have or have not done in life, there is always hope and there is always time to make the intentional choice to pursue a *flourishing* life.

As our journey now arrives in the final part of this book, we are moving to practical application and integration. I am a big believer that information does not bring transformation in anyone's life. Information is just that: *information*. You may ask, then, what does bring transformation? *Integration.* Integration is what brings transformation in our lives.

I simply mean this: what we do with the information we are given in life—how we apply it, how we act on it (or do not act on it), and how we practice it determines what kind of an impact that information makes on our lives. For the remainder of our journey together, I am going to answer the questions "So what?" "What now?" "Now what do I do?" and "What is my next step?" The information in this book is too important to just leave you hanging without any instruction or further direction. Are you ready? I hope you are. Let's begin with the first exercise.

EXERCISE: TELL YOUR STORY

The first thing to do to integrate what you have read in this book into your life is to tell your story. Not anyone else's story—*your* story. Write it down. Throughout this book, I asked you questions to help you integrate what you were learning into your life. If stories, examples, or lessons learned came to mind and you wrote those down as you were reading, what you wrote will serve as great prompts and inputs into your story. If you did not write anything down, consider going back through the book and looking at those questions again. Those questions are there to help you with your story and journey, and those questions are there to help you learn and grow as you integrate the information into your life.

If you do not like to write, then ask someone to write it for you as you tell it. Document your story from the beginning to where you are now. This will help you understand where you have come from, where you are now, and help you determine where you want to go next.

You may say, "I don't like my story" or "My story is too painful. I don't want to tell it or remember it." If the details of parts of your story are too painful or too graphic, then summarize those parts of your story, but please, please do not skip those parts or ignore them. Why? Because you may discover one of two things: (1) You need to remember your past so you can work through your past. You may need to heal. You may need to forgive. (2) Your past hurts, pains, struggles, and failures may reveal ways you can now help others who are dealing with the same things that you dealt with in your story but you came through it. Stronger. Better. Hopeful. Hope-filled. More prepared. And now, the parts of your story that were painful for you may be exactly what someone else is going through now who is struggling, wondering if the pain will ever end, or on the verge of losing all hope.

You may be asking, "How long should my story be?" or "How much time should I spend writing my story?" It is difficult to give you an objective, concrete answer to this question because each person and each person's story is unique to them. This uniqueness is why sharing your story is so important: there is only **one** you! Here are some guidelines to help you with your story.

1. **Format**
   a. If you enjoy writing, consider writing your story in prose by starting at the beginning and writing as many details of your life as you can remember. This may take you some time, so I would encourage you that if you get bogged down or tired of writing, do it in small bite-size chunks. Write for a specific amount of time (e.g., fifteen or thirty minutes, or maybe just five or ten minutes), or write a certain number of words (e.g., write 250 words

a day, or 500, or whatever number makes sense to you) and then stop. This will help prevent you from getting tired of writing (or getting tired of your story!) and may help you if you start to get bogged down. It will also allow you to move on to the other exercises and avoid getting stuck in one exercise for too long.

   b. If you do not enjoy writing, consider these alternatives:

      i. Put your story in outline format and use short sentences that will prompt your memory as to what that means to you in your story.

      ii. Use bullet points that are meaningful to you that will remind you of parts of your story.

      iii. Relate your story to a journey with various mile markers relating to significant events in your own life. I recommend using at least three mile markers related to three significant events in your life.

      iv. Consider artifacts, pictures, or treasures you have in your life and the memories and stories associated with them. Use these to help tell your story. For example, if you enjoy traveling, you may consider using your passport and sharing stories from the places you have been and the impact those travels had on your life.

      v. Tell your story to someone else and have them write it for you.

      vi. Dictate your story to a recording device and have someone write it or use an online service that could transcribe it.

2. Length

   a. There is no correct or incorrect answer when it comes to documenting your story. If you write your story in prose, it may be a couple of pages to many pages. That is great! If you write your story in outline or bullet points, your story may be a couple of pages or less than a page. That is also great!

b. The point in documenting your story is not how long or short it is. The point is this: that you took the time to document your story! This is important because...

   i. It will help you better understand yourself and know who you are.

   ii. It will help your spouse and kids (or your friends and extended family, if you don't have a spouse or kids) better understand you and who you are, which is invaluable in building healthy, growing relationships.

   iii. It will help others as you share your story with them about your journey in life.

c. Remember, there is only ONE you! The world needs to know your story because there will never again be a YOU on the face of the earth.

3. **Evaluate Your Story as a Whole**

After you draft your story, do the following:

a. Look for specific examples throughout your story of times when your life was *diminishing*, *surviving*, *striving*, *thriving*, and *flourishing*. Use the model and the definitions of each of the characteristics to help you as evaluate your story.

b. Be honest about your *current* story. Where are you on the model? Are you *flourishing*? Wonderful! Keep doing whatever you are doing. If you are not *flourishing*, do you want to be? Then whatever level you are now, examine the *barriers* and the *accelerators* at the level and ask yourself two questions:

   i. What is keeping me from moving up to the next level (or higher)? In other words, what are the *barriers* that are keeping me from moving?

   ii. What could help me move to the next level? In other

words, what are the *accelerators* that could help me move further in my journey?

Do this for each level where you want to learn, grow, change, and move.

c. If living a *flourishing* life is where you want to be, then do not stop until you have identified all the *barriers* and the *accelerators* between where you are now and where you want to be. For example, if you are at the *thriving* level now, evaluate the *barriers* that are keeping you from *flourishing* as well as the *accelerators* that could help you move from *thriving* to *flourishing*. If you are at the *surviving* level and you want to live at the *flourishing* level, then evaluate the *barriers* and *accelerators* at your current level, *surviving*, as well as the *striving* and *thriving* levels. Do not stop evaluating until you have thoroughly identified all the *barriers* that could keep you from moving to the level you desire.

   i. Then develop a plan to overcome or mitigate those *barriers*. At the same time, identify all the *accelerators* that could help propel you to the level you desire.

   ii. Then develop a plan to implement those *accelerators*.

d. Chart your journey over time.

   i. Using your story, make a chart of where you were at each level of the model throughout your journey. Start with the beginning of your story and draw a line that moves up and down throughout your journey that follows the levels of the model.

      a. When were you at the *diminishing* level in your story? What were the characteristics and feelings you were experiencing?

      b. When were you at the *surviving* level in your story? What were the characteristics and feelings you were experiencing?

      c. When were you at the *striving* level in your story? What were the characteristics and feelings you were experiencing?

      d. When were you at the *thriving* level in your story? What were the characteristics and feelings you were experiencing?

      e. When were you at the *flourishing* level in your story? What were the characteristics and feelings you were experiencing?

  ii. Then look at the times you were at the same levels and the characteristics and feelings you were experiencing. Do you notice anything in common, patterns, or shared feelings when you were at the same level throughout your story? Make a note of those similarities in your feelings and experiences throughout your story. The next time you identify one or more of these feelings or experiences, it may help you identify what level you are currently experiencing. Then you can make the intentional choice to stay at that level or choose to take steps to move in the direction you desire to move.

  iii. Remember, everyone's story is a journey and is never a straight line. Ever. Evaluate the trendline of your story. Does your journey have a trendline that tilts upward over the course of your journey? Then you are on the path toward living an intentional and purposeful life. Is your trendline flat or tilted downward over the course of your journey? Evaluate where you want to be using the resources in this book, and then intentionally plot a course to reverse the trendline of your journey.

Telling and documenting your story and then evaluating your story in this way will help you evaluate your life's story *as a whole.*

The next chapter will help you evaluate your life's story *by role*. Doing this analysis *as a whole* and by *role* will give you the most complete information possible and the most holistic evaluation possible. Remember, the goal is the *integration* of information that can lead to *transformation* of your life—intentionally choosing to pursue a life that is *flourishing.*

CHAPTER 15

Evaluate Your Life by Role

IN THE PRIOR chapter, we learned how your story will help you evaluate where you are *as a whole.* Now let's take apart your life and evaluate the *roles* you have in your life. Here is what I mean by "roles": any significant function or part that you play in your life. Examples could be spouse, parent, child, sibling, employee, employer, boss, leader, teacher, volunteer, coach, or whatever other *role* you identify. Look at the graphic below to get a feel for what I mean.

This graphic is a simple graphic to help you evaluate your life by role. The different shading in the diagram is merely a way to show differentiation among the various roles you have in life. If you prefer a graphic with no shading or with colors, choose whatever graphic and colors you prefer. The important thing is to choose a graphic that makes sense to you as you complete this exercise.

Important steps to know as you put together your analysis by *role*:

YOUR LIFE BY ROLE

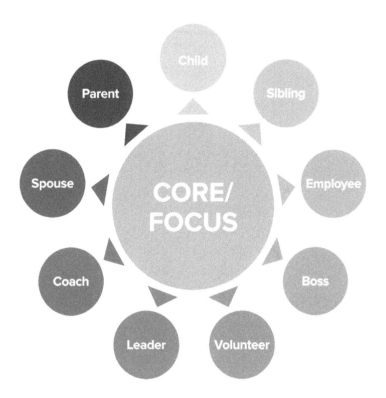

1. **Start with the center circle.** The center circle is NOT a role; it is your core, your center, your "true north," your basic assumption about life, or your fundamental focus in life (hence the arrows pointing out from the center circle). If those descriptions don't fit you, then use whatever description you prefer. These descriptions like "core," "center," or "focus" simply mean your *foundation*. What you build everything else on in your life. For you, that could be "family," or it may be "honesty" or "integrity" or "excellence in all things." For others, it may be "God" or "My relationship with God" (for me, in case you were won-

dering, it is this: "Jesus Christ is exactly who He said He was"—I am basing my entire existence on this foundation for my life). What is the fundamental purpose that everything else flows from in your life? I encourage you to be honest with what is at your *core* now. Then, when you get to Step 4, be honest with yourself about the *core* or *focus* you desire to have for your life. What you have at your *core* now may be exactly what you desire for your future, and that is great; however, if you desire to make a change, Steps 4 and 5 walk you through how to start thinking about changing the *core* for your life.

2. **Develop your own list of** roles. I used circles as one way to evaluate the various *roles* you have in your life. Use whatever format you want that makes sense to you. Draw your diagram based on the number of *roles* you identify in your life.

3. **Fill out the circles around the center first.** After you have your list of the *roles* you have in your life, rate them one *role* at a time from *diminishing*, to *surviving*, to *striving*, to *thriving*, to *flourishing*. After you evaluate each *role*, refer to the diagram and the steps below for how to proceed.

4. **Core shift.** Above are two diagrams. Both have the same roles around the outside. The difference is what is at the core. As you look at the diagram, think about what priorities and how this person would evaluate their life by role. For example, in the example with "Career" in the center, every role would be evaluated through the lens of "How is this role either helping or hindering my career-first focus?" In the other graphic with "Family" at the center, every role would be evaluated through the lens of "How is this role either helping or hindering my family-first focus?" As you can imagine, how this person would evaluate each role— along with the *barriers* and *accelerators* in each role—from

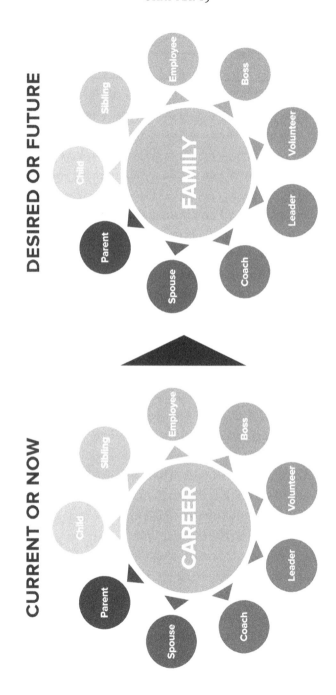

diminishing to *flourishing* would be fundamentally different based on the core focus and prioritizing of this person's life. This would be especially true if the person spent much of his or her life focused on "Career" and now desires to make changes, including a new core focus on "Family." There are many reasons an example like this could become reality. For example, maybe the person realized the sacrifice of time and relationship made in the spouse or parent or friend roles in pursuit of "Career" and now this person seeks to change that by prioritizing "Family" above all else. Another example could be a sudden or a tragic trauma, such as divorce, death, illness, or loss of job that created a "wake-up call" where this person realized that prioritizing "Career" above all else was a much greater cost or sacrifice than they may have realized and now change is both necessary and desired. There are many other examples that a shift in priority like this—or any other shift in priority— could happen.

5. **Draw a second diagram.** Use the same *roles* as in your first diagram but now with a different *core* or *center* or *focus* of your life. Does this change how you evaluate these *roles* as you put together your plan to intentionally pursue *flourishing* in each *role*? **Note:** If your center focus and priority in your first diagram is what you desire it to be, keep the core focus and priority in both diagrams. Your focus is not as much on changing your core and your life prioritization; your focus is on growing in your roles to *flourishing.*

6. **Put together your plan.** Assemble your plan by *role* to eliminate *barriers* or utilize the *accelerators* at each level of the model to pursue *flourishing* in each role. Use your first model as your "here" and your second model as your "there." Then evaluate what it will take, by *role*, to get from "here" to "there" as you evaluate the *barriers* and

the *accelerators* to move in each role. As you put together your plan—especially if you change your "core focus" and life prioritization—you may come to this realization: you may need to eliminate a *role* temporarily or permanently to create time and space for you to grow in another *role*. If you come to that reality, that is great! It means you are facing reality and growing in the knowledge that to pursue a *flourishing* life in all areas, it often means that you need to pursue *less* to experience *more*. The older I get, the more this reality becomes true. At first, I did not like accepting this reality; however, as time went on and I began practicing pursuing and having *less*, I began to experience *more*. I know the same will be true for you as well!

Now that you have evaluated your life by *role* and *as a whole*, let's look at some other tools that may be useful to you in your journey. The next chapter will provide you with additional tools to assist you along your journey.

CHAPTER 16

Three Exercises
on Your Journey

IN THIS CHAPTER, I want to provide you with three different tools you can use on your journey to further integrate what we have been discussing through these pages. I present to you three assessments that are outstanding in helping you grow in self-awareness, which is something we discussed earlier at a high level. Growing in self-awareness will help you grow in your ability to use the Flourishing Life Model more thoroughly.

As you grow in self-awareness, you will grow in the ability to view yourself honestly—your strengths AND your weaknesses; your good points AND your challenging points; what you do very well AND what you do not do well. The better you know yourself, the more you will know what to say no to in life, as well as what to say yes to. Knowing yourself will also allow you the opportunity to invite others along on your journey who can help you know yourself even better, as well as help point out your blind spots that could cause serious hurt to you and to others around you.

Please Note: I highly recommend the use of assessments but with this caveat. When you research these assessments, choose an organization or a consultant who will provide you with an in-person thorough debrief *in addition to* the written report that comes with most assessments. Please do not just choose the free version or the easiest-to-access version unless you know someone who is a certified trainer and can provide you with a debrief and interpretation of your results. The reason for my caution is that I have experienced untrained facilitators who, as well-intentioned as they may be, do not understand how to properly communicate the results of assessments. As a result, untrained facilitators often have errors in their interpretation, or worse, they communicate results or implications from the results that may be hurtful or damaging. For example, I have witnessed untrained facilitators make comments like, "You are this way or that way, and you will never change" or "Because you are this way, you can never do this or think this way or ever achieve success in certain areas." Assessments are never meant to limit, diminish, or put a false "lid" on you, your potential, or your capacity. If you would like further information on assessments or have any questions, please feel free to contact me. My contact information is in the About the Author section toward the end of this book.

DISC

The first assessment that I pursued formal training in and one of my favorite assessments to this day is the DISC assessment. At a summary level, the DISC assessment evaluates four basic personalities, along with their basic behavioral indicators. Here is a high-level summary of the four basic personalities:

- D. Dominant, Driven Personality Type
- I. Inspirational, Influential Personality Type

- S. Steady, Stable Personality Type
- C. Conscientious, Cautious Personality Type

In addition, the assessment determines your personality "blend" because everyone is a blend of all four personality types (higher in some and lower in others).

The DISC assessment was one of the first assessments that Tiffani and I took when we were married. The results were nothing less than remarkable. Tiffani and I are opposites of each other. Fundamentally, we knew we were different, which is what initially attracted us to each other. But just as opposites often attract, those differences that once attracted us often turn to frustration and aggravation. As the saying goes, "Opposites attract! And then opposites attack!" Without a framework to understand our differences, our marriage quickly moved from *thriving* (I do not know many marriages that would experience *flourishing* in its first year or two—I am sure there are exceptions, but I believe they would be just that: the exception) to *surviving*, and we were frustrated. Over time, the more we grew in self-awareness and learned our wiring, the more we grew in others-awareness, and the more our marriage relationship grew. By intentionally choosing to learn and to grow, our marriage grew to the *flourishing* level. My hope for you is that regardless of whether you are married or not, you will grow in this same self- and others-awareness so you can grow in individual and relational health toward a *flourishing* life.

MYERS-BRIGGS (MBTI)

Myers-Briggs (MBTI) is another assessment that helps you grow in self- and others-awareness. Whereas DISC focuses on personality traits, characteristics, and behaviors, MBTI focuses more on *preferences*. A high-level overview for you of these preferences is below. MBTI focuses on four dimensions with two preferences on each dimension. In each dimension, you choose the one that is most like you. You may identify characteristics of both preferences in each dimension, and that is fine; however, to determine your MBTI four-letter combination, you would choose the preference that describes you the most, even if the difference is not much. Considering there are four dimensions with two preferences on each dimension, it gives a total of sixteen possible four-letter MBTI combinations.

- The first dimension is "energy" by evaluating if you prefer to recharge your proverbial batteries either *Internally* or *Externally*. If you prefer to recharge *Internally* (some versions use "Introvert"), you prefer to recharge by being alone or engage in an activity with close family or friends, engage in contemplative thought, or by reading. If you prefer to recharge *Externally* (some versions use "Extrovert"), you prefer to engage with other people either in conversation or in activities, you enjoy talking, and you usually enjoy meeting new people.
- The second dimension is "information processing" by evaluating if you prefer to evaluate information through *Sensing* (think five senses) or through *Intuition* (think "gut feeling"). If you prefer to evaluate information through *Sensing*, you prefer a more systematic evaluation of facts, figures, and concrete research. If you prefer *Intuition*, you prefer to trust your gut in making connections between your past and current experiences.
- The third dimension is "decision making" by evaluating if you prefer to make decisions via *Thinking* (think logic) or *Feeling* (think emotion or impact). If you prefer *Thinking*, you prefer a logical, systematic approach to making decisions. If you prefer *Feeling*, you prefer to consider emotions and impact on people and relationships in your approach

to making decisions. Most people use both but prefer to start with one preference and finish with the other preference (the one you start with is the one that determines your MBTI letter—Thinking (T) or Feeling (F)—for the "decision making" dimension).

- The final dimension is "organization" by evaluating if you prefer *Judging* (think organized, planned, systems, convergent thinking) or *Perceiving* (think spontaneous, open-ended, flexible, divergent thinking). If you prefer *Judging*, you prefer to be organized, utilize systems, adhere to a fixed schedule, and have detailed plans. If you prefer *Perceiving*, you prefer spontaneity, flexible systems, varied schedules, and open-ended plans.

How does this all relate to your journey to *flourishing*? Your journey is bound to be a journey with other people. The more you understand your and others' preferences and what makes you and others tick, the more you can intentionally build deep, healthy relationships. This directly contributes to your well-being and to your journey toward *flourishing* in your relationships.

ENNEAGRAM

Enneagram is an amazing journey of self-awareness and self-discovery. Enneagram examines motivation and what drives people to behave or not behave in certain ways. Using a numbering system from 1 to 9, Enneagram "lives" with you on your journey. Yes, there are Enneagram assessments out there that will provide you with a number from 1 to 9 and a definition of what your number means. However, I recommend that you take time to read books and study what the nine numbers mean, learn about the underlying motivations of each of the nine numbers, and identify for yourself where you see yourself in the nine numbers. Do this prior to taking an assessment. If you want to start with an assessment (like I did), that is fine; however, please then spend time with a trained facilitator and coach in Enneagram. I would also highly recommend the following books by Suzanne Stabile and Jerome Wagner, PhD—two of my favorite experts and teachers of Enneagram.

- By Suzanne Stabile, I recommend the books *The Road Back to You* (coauthored with Ian Morgan Cron) and *The Path between Us.*
- By Jerome Wagner, PhD, I recommend the books *The Enneagram Spectrum of Personality Styles* and *Nine Lenses of the World.*

How does Enneagram apply to your journey toward a *flourishing* life? It is the same answer as before: it will be difficult—if not impossible—to make intentional decisions to pursue a *flourishing* life if you do not first know who you are. The fundamental point throughout the pages of our journey together has been to know yourself so you can evaluate the life you have now versus the life you intentionally desire to have. This evaluation starts with the foundation of knowing yourself.

There are other assessments I highly recommend that provide wonderful insights and growth; however, the three I have listed here provide you with both a great start and a solid foundation as you continue your journey of growing in self-awareness, others-awareness, and relational health. The next chapter will provide you with one final exercise to help you on your journey in choosing the path of a *flourishing* life.

CHAPTER 17

Game-Changing Questions

A S OUR JOURNEY draws near to the end, I want to leave you with one final exercise to do to help you integrate what we have been discussing during our journey. I call this the Game-Changing Questions Exercise. I will give you the questions and then spend a little time explaining why both of these are game-changing questions on your journey to *flourishing*.

1. Game-Changing Question #1: *What is YOUR why?*
2. Game-Changing Question #2: *What will be YOUR legacy?*

Game-Changing Question #1: *What is YOUR why?* Let's start with the first game-changing question, "What is YOUR why?" I first mentioned this in Part I, but it is an important part of assessing yourself on your journey to *flourishing*, so I reiterate it here. To unpack this question, consider these follow-up questions:

- "Why do you exist?"

- "What is your purpose?"
- "Why did God create you, put you here on this earth, at this time in history?"

Since I can remember, I have been passionately pursuing the answer to these questions, as well as "What is God's will for my life?" and "Why am I here?" I have read books, I have interviewed experts, and I have researched this extensively. Based on this, it would be a safe assumption to conclude that I found the answers to the questions I have been seeking for over three decades, correct? Although it may be a safe assumption to make, it would be an inaccurate assumption because I do not know the answers; however, along the journey, I did make profound discoveries. First, God's will is a difficult concept to grasp. Why? Because whenever I think about God's will and whenever I have asked others about their pursuit of knowing God's will, the context is often about knowing what God wants me and others to *DO*. And that is the rub—we all want to know what we are supposed to DO. If we only knew exactly and beyond any doubt what it is that we are supposed to DO in life, we would be happy and experience a *flourishing* life, correct? There is no straightforward way to answer this question because the answer to that question is yes, and it is also no.

I have learned this in my decades' pursuit of knowing God's will for my life: *God is infinitely more interested in Who over What.* In other words, God cares about me as a person and who I am becoming infinitely more than He cares about what I DO. And the same applies to you—God cares infinitely more about WHO you are than WHAT you DO. As a result of this, I have come to this conclusion: if I am in a relationship with God and pursuing a life where I am becoming the best version of who I am created to be—aka a *flourishing* life—then what I DO is much less important.

My why is now centered on pursuing a *flourishing* life by pursuing what God has uniquely created, equipped, and prepared me to

DO. I am excited to be on this journey, fully knowing that most of the time, both my faith and my trust will be tested to the limits. I want to encourage you to do the same. Pursue a *flourishing* life by growing in your self-awareness, pursue what you are passionate about, and pursue what you are uniquely created, equipped, and prepared to DO.

Game-Changing Question #2: *What will be YOUR legacy?* The second game-changing question is, "What will be YOUR legacy?" To unpack this question, consider this follow-up question: "When you look back on your life at the end of it—hopefully at a ripe old age—what will those closest to you say your life was all about?"

In the early days of building my family business, I worked part time as a youth pastor for Youth-for-Christ and then as my church's high school youth pastor. I mentioned earlier that every year, usually in October, I would do a series on living life to the fullest, what happens after death, and other related topics. I know it may sound morbid, but these topics would routinely get the best feedback of the year. One exercise I would have the students do is to get into small groups of four to five students and imagine they are at the end of their life—a long, well-lived life—and then look back on their lives. I asked the students to write their epitaph or obituary and then share it with their small group. Some students, as you can imagine, put together silly—sometimes witty and funny—epitaphs. Other students put together very well-thought-through epitaphs and obits—some of which I still remember over twenty-five years later.

Because the response to this exercise was so profound, I thought I would start using it whenever I would speak to groups of executives and senior Leaders. The response? Completely unpredictable. After the sessions were over, I had many leaders come up to me with tears coming down their faces as they shared what they had written, but more importantly, the changes they were committing to making in their lives to make their families a greater priority, to take better care of themselves physically, to get back into church, and the stories went on and on. It was remarkable. It was life changing. It was transformative.

I want to encourage you to do the same exercise. Regardless of your age, imagine the end of your life—hopefully, many years from now—and imagine looking back. Then ask and answer these questions for you:

- What are three descriptions of you and your life that you most desire your spouse, children, and closest friends to say about you at your funeral?
- What would those closest to you say defined you and that you valued in life?
- What would people write about you in your obituary or write on your epitaph?

The answer to these questions gets to the heart of *"What will YOUR legacy be?"*

- For some, you will discover that your journey is on track and there is little to no change needed on your life's journey. This exercise will confirm for you that you are pursuing and living a *flourishing* life.
- For others, you may discover this exercise provides a wake-up call, and you may realize that if you do not make course corrections—perhaps significant course corrections—you may wind up at the end of your life's journey with regret and remorse. Your current path in life may be *thriving* on the outside but barely *surviving* or even *diminishing* on the inside.

Whatever the case for you, this exercise is one of the most powerful exercises you can do to see if your current path is leading to the end destination that you desire or if your journey needs adjustments.

Before we move on, a particularly important question you may be asking now or may ask at some point on your journey: *What happens if I lose my way or my journey goes in the wrong direction?* This is a terrific question! The journey to a *flourishing* life requires you to pull off the road occasionally and evaluate where you have been, where you are currently, and where you are going. If you do not like what you see, you can adjust your journey. Please know this: Your journey is not so set or predetermined that you cannot make adjustments along the way!

Now onto the conclusion: a summary of our time together and a final call to action.

CONCLUSION

A s we arrive at the end of our journey, let's briefly review where we have been together. I will finish by asking you the same question that I started with: *Are you satisfied with your life?* Your answer may be, "Yes!" Then I say to you, "Wonderful! Keep pursuing and living your best life!" Your answer may be, "Yes and no." I say to you, "Wonderful! Keep pursuing those areas of your life that you are satisfied with and make the intentional choice to change those areas of your life where you are *unsatisfied*." Or perhaps your answer is a resounding "No!" I say to you, "Wonderful! Please do not wait another minute to make the intentional choices to pursue change—to pursue a *flourishing* life that leads to true *satisfaction* in your life."

I promised you at the beginning that I would not give you formulas, pithy solutions, or empty promises, and I am not about to go back on my word as we near the end of our journey together. So please hear me when I say this and please do not miss this: if you are *unsatisfied* with your life—whether *as a whole* or in certain *roles*—or the current trajectory of your life, there is another way. This journey is NOT easy, but it is so very worth it! This journey will mean facing some of your biggest fears, it will mean facing your insecurities, it will mean having self-doubt, it will mean growing in self-awareness and others-awareness, and it will mean having to endure others around you—maybe even family and friends—giving you that raised eyebrow, scrunched face, pursed-lips look of "What in the world are you thinking and doing?"

Sound like a fun journey? Unbelievably, it is! How can I say everything I just said and then say the journey is fun? You must think I am a complete whack job. Possibly. But I will let my therapist decide that. *Diminished. Surviving. Striving. Thriving. Flourishing.* I have experienced them all. Chances are, so have you and many others you know. I would go out on a limb and say that you have experienced each of these at least once in life, whether in your life *as a whole* or in certain *roles* in your life. You are "fearfully and wonderfully made," as Psalm 139 declares.[24] You are created uniquely and beautifully. You are created with unique gifts and skills. Therefore, it is vital for you to become the best and fullest version of you because there is only one YOU. The world needs all of you—full-on—because there is and only ever will be ONE YOU!

Two of the worst feelings in the world are those of helplessness and hopelessness. I am convinced that no one must experience either one of these feelings—at least not permanently. Throughout my life, I have experienced each level of the Flourishing Life Model. Although I do not have all the answers to the complex questions that life has to offer—not even close—I do have something to offer. I offer you this wisdom: The *thriving* life is a good life to live, but it does not compare to the *flourishing* life, not in the least. Experiencing a *flourishing* life is something that is best described by living it and knowing it when you see it.

I shared with you that Eric Liddell is my human hero, but the reality is this: Jesus is my hero—my only true hero. In the New Testament, Jesus talks about His life and mission. He knew who

---

24   Ps. 139:13–14 (English Standard Version).

He was. He knew His *what*. He knew His *why*. He knew what He believed, why He believed it, and He articulated His vision, mission, beliefs, and values with amazing precision and passion. Jesus said over and over that He came to give life and give it to the fullest—He wants everyone to experience life to the fullest. But He also knew that the path to a full life—a *flourishing* life—was difficult, and many would never experience it. Many, if not most, would say they want to experience a *flourishing* life and even pursue the journey of experiencing a *flourishing* life. But Jesus also knew that there would be obstacles and barriers and counterfeits along the way, and He also knew there would be *accelerators* as well. It is this desire for everyone—and I do mean everyone—to experience life to the fullest, a *flourishing* life, that motivated me to pen the words on the pages you have been reading.

Throughout our journey together through the pages of this book, we explored the Flourishing Life Model. We journeyed together through the levels of the model, starting with *Diminishing*. We learned together that the *Diminishing* level is represented by a mindset of giving up, not trying anymore, and having feelings of hopelessness and helplessness. We moved to the next level of *Surviving* where we learned that *Surviving* is represented by a mindset of doing whatever is necessary to live today, having little consideration for tomorrow, and having feelings that this is all that life has to offer. Our journey then took us to *Striving* where we learned that *Striving* is represented by a mindset of not being satisfied with living day to day by merely *surviving*; trying to better oneself through education, coaching, and intentional learning; and having feelings of a growing hope that tomorrow will be better than today. Next, we were on to *Thriving* where we learned that *Thriving* represented a focus on accumulating wealth, power, position, title, and possessions; having a mindset that one can do whatever one puts his or her mind to doing, and having feelings that one is experiencing his or her best life.

Finally, we arrived at *Flourishing* where we learned that *Thriving* often results in feelings of being *unsatisfied* without really understanding why. We learned that while *Thriving* is a focus inward on oneself, *Flourishing* is a focus outward—on giving back, on investing in others, on pursuing one's passion based on how one is uniquely gifted and equipped. *Flourishing* has the mindset of "surrender," meaning surrendering and being willing to trust God and His plan and calling for one's life, rather than holding on to whatever it is that we thought was important but came to the stark, and often unsettling, realization that one's possessions, money, title, position, and power do not lead to lasting, sustained *satisfaction* with one's life. *Flourishing* is about living out of one's core values and beliefs and living a life that gives back, invests into others, and lives for something greater than oneself. *Flourishing* has the mindset of hope, love, and faith that is integrated throughout one's life both *as a whole* and by *role*.

On our journey, we looked at the power of story—YOUR story. I shared some of my story with the hope that you would also see your own story in some of mine and that would provide you with the hope and the courage to share your own story with others. Our journey then arrived at integration—integration of what we learned along our journey together into your life. We examined examples and exercises to grow in self- and others-awareness, because the journey to a *flourishing* life begins with knowing yourself first and then others second. However, my hope and prayer for you is that your journey has only just begun!

If you want to experience the *flourishing* life, then make the choice to *intentionally pursue* the journey to a *flourishing* life. A simple answer and a simple commitment to make; however, the journey is not as easy as the answer. Why? Because our world, our culture, our society, and our lives are broken. Our society tells us to pursue *more* and *better*, the very definition of a *thriving* life. I mentioned this before, but I will say it again: if you want to live a life that few others are experiencing (aka a *flourishing* life), then you must make the intentional choices that few others are making.

A journey happens one step at a time—putting one foot in front of the other and taking one step and then another. Before you know it, you look behind you, and you realize that you have taken many steps and you are well on your journey. The journey of life is not a straight line, and sometimes it seems as though you are not moving at all. Sometimes the journey is iterative—even covering the same ground you have covered before. If you keep taking steps, you are still moving. Sometimes you must take steps backward to take steps forward in a different, better direction. All of this is okay because with each step you take, you are learning, growing, and figuring out the best path to take on your journey. The thing to realize on your journey is this: *there is hope*. There is always hope.

How about you? What is your path to *flourishing*?

For you, it may not be something as drastic as leaving your job and pursuing something new or something different. But it may be just that. Whatever it is—whether in your current role, a different role, in business, in a nonprofit, in a church, in this country, in another country, on the mission field, in the classroom, in the art room, or in a janitor's closet—take one step and then another. I am a big believer that it is so much better to live life with the knowledge of trying something and experiencing the failure of it not working out than to live life with the regret of never trying at all. If you are afraid of something, name it aloud. Then break it down into simple steps and take the logical and best next step. Do not try to take the next thirty steps; just take the next *ONE* step.

It is the same as trying to eat an elephant (assuming you would ever want to eat one): *one bite at a time*. How do you experience the *flourishing* life? Discover what you are passionate about, what you dream of doing, what you are good at doing, and what others say you do to contribute value to them. Then take one step. Then take another step. It may take 30, 100, or 1,000 steps to reach your dream of a *flourishing* life. Fine! But the only way to get to Step 30, 100, or 1,000 is to take Step 1. The fact you have made it to the end of this book is proof enough for me that you just took Step 1. Congratulations! Step 2? Work through the exercises and examples in Part III of this book. You have invested yourself and your time to read these pages. Invest a little more in yourself and work through the exercises in this section. Continue your journey toward self- and others-awareness and begin to integrate the concepts and what you have learned in these pages into your life. That is Step 2! Step 3, make the intentional choices and decisions necessary to commit to pursuing a *flourishing* life. Step 4 and beyond? That is up to you!

Even though our journey through these pages has ended, please know two things: (1) I am cheering for you and praying for you on your journey! Although I may not know you by name, I know the journey you are about to go on, and I see you, and I am for you all the way. (2) If you would like additional help or resources for your journey, please do not hesitate to contact me. My email is in the About the Author section of this book. I will do whatever I am able to do to support you on your journey toward a *flourishing* life. Now go take a step and then take another step! Your journey toward a *flourishing* life is in front of you.

GRATITUDE

For years, I dreamed of writing a book, but I put it off, saying, "I have no idea where to start." The process has been more challenging and more rewarding than I could have ever imagined. What motivated me to finally start? Certain people believed in me and lovingly nudged me to start writing. Kate Volman with Floyd Consulting implored me for months to start my "vomit draft"—just puking words out onto paper. Thanks, Kate, for the monthly encouragement and challenge to keep writing every day until I was finished. Kate also introduced me to Scribe Media. What a godsend Scribe Media has been. Nathan Allen, once a direct report of mine, left a note and a book on my desk as he departed his job. The note was a thank you note and concluded by saying, "I look forward to reading your book," and the book was *Finish* by Jon Acuff, which wound up being the final catalyst to get me over the mental barrier that writing a book is just too difficult.

Scribe Media. I do not even know where to begin. Mikey Kershisnik, my publishing manager, your Zoom calls and emails kept me moving when I was not sure this was going to ever happen. Nicole Jobe, my editor, "thank you" does not fully express it. The time you took with my original manuscript to fulfill my original vision for this book was nothing less than amazing. Although I was intimidated by all the red lines and the sheer number of comments, your editing, your feedback, your questions, and your guidance has taught me so very much about effective writing. This book would not be here without you! Hal Clifford, thank you for the "crucial conversation." Our conversation prepared me to hold everything loosely and trust the process. Skyler Gray, thank you for lending your creative mind to come up with a much better title than I had originally planned. Jean Nicolas Serna-Hincapie, thank for your efficient and effective managing of this project to the end. Kevin Quach, your genius in designing the covers was truly amazing. Keep using your skills and gifts to make a difference! Braxton Benes, thank you for your eye for quality at the end. You brought this to the next level of excellence with your edits. Ami Hendrickson, you are a gifted copywriter. Thank you for making this project complete by contributing your gifts to the copywriting process. To everyone else at Scribe that I would have loved to have worked with personally, your work was a vital part of the team effort that made this book a reality. Thank you from the bottom of my heart to:

- Design Specialist: Sarafina Riskind
- Manuscript Specialist: Vi La Bianca
- Production Specialist: Benito Salazar
- Publishing Specialist: Robert Roth
- Graphic Designer: Mariano Paniello
- Copy Editor: Laura Cail
- Proofreader: Joyce Li
- The Scribe Impact team

Scribe Team, I would not have been able to do this without you, literally. "Thank you" does not begin to express my gratitude for all of you—as a team and as individuals.

My friends. Your support, encouragement, love, and belief in me was more than I could have ever asked for or imagined. Mike

Kooistra, my dependable, loyal friend for over twenty years. I love you, man. Thank you for everything you do, but thank you for you and your friendship most of all. Scott Pflughoeft, your friendship is a blessing and an encouragement. I am a better man because of your friendship. Jason Slone, thank you for your belief in me and for walking through the "valley of the shadow of death" with me. I am truly grateful. Garrett ("Gary") Cooper, after sharing an office (by choice!) for six years, you still want to be my friend ☺. Thank you for your wisdom, counsel, and feedback during this process. It was invaluable. Verlin Rice, "thank you" is too little for all you have done. Your encouragement, wisdom, and love has been invaluable to Tiffani and me. I can never thank you enough. Gabe Clark, your energy, your vision, and your commitment to Jesus and your family both challenge and inspire me, my friend. Thank you for your unwavering support and encouragement. BG Allen, all the hours on the phone...priceless. I value your wisdom and counsel. More importantly, I value you for being you. Pastor Bill Lyne and Sue Lyne, my church leaders for twenty-nine years, but more importantly, my friends. You believed in a snot-nosed, cocky teenager and gave him an opportunity. All these years later, still not sure what you were thinking! Thank you. David and Jane Foster, it has been a joy to be in relationship with you. Where have the years gone? Thank you for your love and encouragement. Chris Mann, thank you for believing in me and helping me be better. I appreciate you and I am so grateful for our friendship. Chuck Yeager, I love that you have lived enough life to live life without a filter. I value your input and feedback in my life. Chuck Bentley, thank you for writing the Foreword for this book. I am grateful. More importantly, thank you for being an example of living an integrated and flourishing life as an inspiration to many. Thank you for being faithful. Proverbs 27:17 says, "As iron sharpens iron, so one person sharpens another." Each of you sharpens me, and I am truly grateful and blessed. Thank you all for walking with me during this part of my journey. I am cognizant of the sacrifice of time that each of my friends' spouses makes so your husbands can hang out with me. Thank you, Cheryl Kooistra, Wendy Pflughoeft, Aimee Slone, Jennifer Cooper, Pat Rice, Olivia Clark, Angela Allen, Ruth Mann, and Judy Yeager.

My family. To my three kids—I mean, young adults—Quentin, Danielle, and Blake, thank you for your calls and your conversations encouraging your dad to keep pressing on. I do not say it enough: thank you, and I am so very proud of the men and the woman of God you are growing into as you mature. I love each of you very much! To my in-laws, Jack and Monica Cook, without you there is no Tiffani. I am grateful. Thank you for your support and encouragement. And a special thank you to Scotty "the Dood"—the family's hyperactive, hyper-loving goldendoodle with separation anxiety. Thanks for keeping my feet warm while I typed outside on those cool nights because I wasn't allowed to have a cigar in the house.

My bride. To my beautiful bride of over twenty-five years, Tiffani. "Thank you" is only the beginning of the depth of gratitude and love I have for you. I have loved you since we were in third grade, and I will love you to the day we draw our final breath. You believed in me when it seemed like no one else did; you believed in my potential and have been loving me to that potential ever since. The "Lesser Life" is a journey that we affectionately refer to as being full of the unknown, the unexpected, and challenges, but this is a beautiful life because we get to be on this journey together...no matter what in life happens. Thank you for providing the initial sketch that Kevin used to create the final cover of the book. I love it!

My Savior, Jesus. Thank You. Thank You for allowing this dream to become a reality. This entire process is and has been in Your hands. I continue to surrender my life to You and choose a flourishing life daily. You are my Jehovah Jireh.

May everyone who reads this be impacted to intentionally choose to live a *flourishing* life. May it be so!

Lightning Source UK Ltd.
Milton Keynes UK
UKHW010050111022
410273UK00008B/83